SUM TOTAL OF HUMAN HAPPINESS

Other Titles of Interest from St. Augustine's Press

SUM TOTAL OF HUMAN HAPPINESS

JAMES V. SCHALL, S.J.

ST. AUGUSTINE'S PRESS
South Bend, Indiana
2006

Manufactured in the United States of America.

1 2 3 4 5   11 10 09 08 07 06

Library of Congress Cataloging in Publication Data
Schall, James V.
    The sum total of human happiness / by James V. Schall –
    1st ed.
      p. cm.
    Includes bibliographical references and index.
    ISBN 1-58731-810-5 (hardcover : alk. paper)
    1. Happiness. 2. Joy. 3. Ontology. I.Title.
  B187.H3S33 2005
  110 – dc22   2005005587

x *The paper used in this publication meets the minimum requirements
of the American National Standard for Information Sciences –
Permanence of Paper for Printed Materials, ANSI Z39.48–1984.*

St. Augustine's Press
www.staugustine.com

"But when we return from error, it is by knowledge that we return."
– Augustine, Confessions, XI, 8.

"Pippin glanced in some wonder at the face [of Gandalf] now close beside his own, for the sound of that laugh had been gay and merry. Yet in the wizard's face he saw at first only lines, of care and sorrow; though as he looked more intently he perceived that under all there was a great joy: a fountain of mirth enough to set the kingdom laughing, were it to gush forth."
– J. R. R. Tolkien, The Return of the King
(New York: Ace, n.d.), 26–17.

"Therefore, as the divine wisdom is the cause of the distinction of things for the sake of the perfection of the universe, so it is the cause of inequality. For the universe would not be perfect if only one grade of goodness were found in things."
– Thomas Aquinas, Summa Theologiae, I, 47, 2.

"History as a whole is the struggle between love and the inability to love, between love and the refusal to love. This is also, in fact, something we are experiencing again today, when man's independence is pushed to the point where he says: I don't want to love at all, because then I make myself dependent, and that contradicts my freedom. Indeed, love means being dependent on something that perhaps can be taken away from me, and it therefore introduces a huge risk of suffering into my life."
– Josef Cardinal Ratzinger, Salt of the Earth
(San Francisco: Ignatius, 1997) 282–83.

"Joy, which was the small publicity of the pagan, is the gigantic secret of the Christian. . . . There was something that He [Christ] covered constantly by abrupt silence or impetuous isolation. There was some one thing that was too great for God to show us when He walked upon our earth; and I have sometimes fancied that it was His mirth."
– G. K. Chesterton, Orthodoxy
(Garden City, N.Y.: Doubleday Image [1908] 1959), 160.

Socrates: "Well, then, he must take the longer road and put as much effort into learning as into physical training, for otherwise . . . he would never reach the goal of the most important subject and the most appropriate one for him to learn."

Adeimantus: "Aren't these virtues, then, the most important things? Is there anything even more important than justice and the other virtues we discussed?"

Socrates: "There is something more important. However, even forr the virtues themselves, it isn't enough to look at a mere sketch . . . while neglecting the most complete account. It's ridiculous, isn't it, to strain every nerve to attain the utmost exactness and clarity about other things of little value and not to consider the most important things worthy of the greatest exactness?"

Adeimantus: "It certainly is."

– Plato, The Republic, VII, 504d.

Acknowledgments

The author would like to thank the following journals for permission: Chapter I, *Canadian C. S. Lewis Journal*; Chapter III, *Logos*; Chapter IV, Fellowship of Catholic Scholars *Newsletter*; Chapter V, *The Aquinas Review*; Chapter VI, *Catholic Dossier*; Chapter VII, *Homiletic and Pastoral Review*; Chapter IX, *The New Oxford Review*; Chapter X, *Vital Speeches*; Chapter XI, *Modern Age*; Chapter XII, *New Blackfriars*; and Chapter XIV, *The Saint Austin Review*.

Table of Contents

Introduction

BETWEEN TWO WALKS

The chapters that follow in these pages will be more intelligible if the reader begins with a slow and careful examination, yes, rumination, of the six short citations found in the very beginning of this book. Here are passages from a German theologian, from the great Augustine and Aquinas. Socrates is there, as are Tolkien and Chesterton, favorites of mine. The spirit of this book is found here in these sentences. The book's title, *The Sum Total of Human Happiness*, is itself related to Samuel Johnson, the great English lexicographer and philosopher. It is a happy, yet unusual, phrase. Johnson simply delighted in things, and we should follow him in this delight. We are not here concerned with the happiness of God unless, perhaps, this happiness is also that from which we ourselves ultimately arise and to which we return.

Surrounding all that is written here are two walks, wonderful walks, one from France to Italy, the other in Sussex in England, walks taken by Hilaire Belloc, the English writer, in 1901 and 1902, more than a hundred years before our time. Here we are presented with the notion of "being happy in this life," but with a caveat, namely, of "being reasonably happy." The limits do not necessarily come from the happiness but from "this life," as it is called. Belloc understood that there were what he called "enduring things." This is a marvelous phrase – "enduring things."

The most unsettling thing about our existence is not that we suffer, not that we fail to accomplish what we might, not even that we sin. Rather it is that, in spite of all this darker side of reality which we do not deny, we exist for joy and for happiness. The classical philosophers knew of this end, as it were, this happiness, but they were not clear in what it might consist. They could, however, exclude certain things that certainly did not belong to it. Their philosophy, unlike much of modernity, was not, in principle, closed in on itself. The classical writers were, if we might put it this way, open to suggestions. And the suggestions did come. Thus, one of the themes of this book is precisely how things fit together, even the things of revelation. When thinking of such things, it is not a bad idea to begin and to end with a walk during which we ponder our being. We too can be peripatetics – those who, while walking about, seek to know, to know the truth of things. We will touch on walking and seeing and letting our souls be open to *what is*.

What might we find in these six initial passages? In the *Republic*, Socrates told the young Adeimantus, the permanent representative, along with his brother, Glaucon, of all potential philosophers, that, while virtue is important, it does not stand by itself. Somehow, it itself is ordered to something higher than itself. There are indeed things of "little value," many things, good things. They are not to be deprecated. Nothing is too small to pass our notice, if we will. We should rejoice, as Aquinas intimated, that there are many things and not just one thing. We have, indeed, the power to reject all else by choosing only ourselves, to choose a freedom that has room for ourselves alone. Yet, it

is a suffocating, desperate thing to allow no genuine otherness into our world.

Augustine uses a phrase about "turning" from error,
almost as if this turning is what we would want to do but
we are not quite sure how. And how are we to make this
turning? Through knowledge, through philosophy and the
love of the *things that are*. And to what end does knowledge
lead? To the truth, of course. We find, with Socrates, that
to speak of the highest things, we must also speak of truth.

And yet, truth is often present to us as something stark,
something almost frightening, and it is frightening, if we
do not also choose it. But it is not so in itself. We are made
to know and to know the truth, the truth of what is not ourselves, the truth of ourselves. There is, likewise, something
strange, unsettling about joy and mirth, things that seem
to follow on our knowing the truth. Truth is to say of *what
is*, that it is, as Plato memorably put it. We cannot set out
to obtain joy as if it were the direct object of our search. It
is, as Josef Pieper will say, a "by-product," the result of
knowing and doing the truth.[1] But joy is there; it follows
truth and right.

Contrary to all external appearances, Gandalf, the great
Wizard in the *Lord of the Rings*, was perceived as bearing
in his soul "a great joy and a fountain of mirth." How
strange, yet how appropriate, it is that this "mirth" is the
one thing that Christ did not reveal to us. It was not that
He did not also possess this mirth, even in his Passion. Yet,
as Chesterton recognizes, we would be disheartened to
know of the fullness of God's mirth before we are prepared
to receive it. The history of the world, in one sense, is this
very preparation for mirth, for everlasting joy, but at best
we only see it as in a "glass, darkly," to use St. Paul's
famous phrase.

1 *Josef Pieper – an Anthology* (San Francisco: Ignatius Press, 1989),
  32–39.

Between Belloc's two walks, we find the classic things of our kind to consider – but to consider with a certain lightsomeness, a certain delight. Our existence is sober in many ways, to be sure, but it is also amusing. It is no accident that we are the beings who also laugh. But in the end, what we seek is not merely the "one thing necessary," though we seek that too, but, in a proper order, all the things *that are*, be they necessary or not. Nothing exists that is not good. *Omne ens est bonum*. We exist not just because of the highest goods, but because of all goods. We ourselves belong to this latter category of things that need not be but nonetheless *are*. It is a cause both of wonder and yes of rejoicing. Of such things we are concerned here.

Chapter I

THE PATH TO ROME: BELLOC'S WALK A CENTURY LATER
On Being "Reasonably" Happy
in This Life

"To every honest reader that may purchase, hire, or receive this book, and to the reviewers also (to whom it is of triple profit), greeting – and whatever else can be had for nothing."
> – Hilaire Belloc, The Path to Rome[1]

"And now all you people reading, may have read, or shall in the future read this my many-sided but now ending book; and all of you also that in the mysterious designs of Providence may not be fated to read it for some very long time to come . . . the time is come when I must bid you farewell."
> – Hilaire Belloc, The Path to Rome *(264)*

I.

In the Year 1901, the English essayist, historian, poet, sailor, and traveler Hilaire Belloc (1870–1953) decided to

---

1 Hilaire Belloc, *The Path to Rome* (Garden City, N.Y.: Doubleday Image, [1902] 1956), 7. (Henceforth, the page numbers will be cited in parentheses immediately after citation in the text without further identification.)

make a pilgrimage from Toul in France, scene of his military training in the French army, to the Eternal City. He chose a direct path to Rome, or at least as direct as the mountains and rivers of Europe would allow him to walk that distance in a straight line. He vowed – for a pilgrimage was a sacred event in the tradition of Christian men – that he would walk every step of the way, in the same boots with which he began, that he would hear Mass every morning, that he would not take a wheeled vehicle, and that he would arrive in Rome on the Feast of Sts. Peter and Paul (29 June) in time for Mass in the great Basilica of St. Peter's.

Needless to say, Belloc broke all the elements of his vow except its final one. He did make it to Rome, though when he arrived, he told us practically nothing of what he saw there.

> "Well, as a pilgrimage cannot be said to be over till the first Mass is heard in Rome, I have twenty minutes to add to my book." So, passing an Egyptian obelisk which the great Augustus had nobly dedicated to the Sun, I entered. . . . LECTOR: "But do you intend to tell us nothing of Rome?" AUCTOR: "Nothing, dear Lector." LECTOR: "Tell me at least one thing; did you see the Coliseum?" AUCTOR: ". . . I entered a café at the right hand of a very narrow, long, straight street, called for bread, coffee, and brandy . . ." (269).

Belloc then writes as his concluding words in the book, presumably from the same café, a "Dithyrambic Epithalamium on Threnody," the concluding lines of which read: "Across the valleys and the high-land / With all the world on either hand / Drinking when I had a mind to, / Singing when I felt inclined to; / Nor ever turned my face to home / Till I had slaked my heart at Rome." The Lector calls this "doggerel," but Belloc does not mind. His walk is ended, his vow completed.

The Path to Rome is thus not about Rome but about

getting there through a Europe that reflects Rome at every step. Belloc passed along the Rhone, over the Alps, through Switzerland, the Apennines, and into the Italian plains and cities on his path. As he went along, he told us much. He told us especially much of himself. Belloc, I think, could see more about something than most of us even when we are looking at the same thing. It is not merely that our memory is a function of what we see, so likewise is our hope, so likewise is our present being.

Not unlike Plato in *The Apology of Socrates*, Belloc was conscious of the fact that this account of his walk would be read down the ages. In this sense, his "path" is a walk we can all take. Because he recounted his trek in a book, we can still take the same walk. We could not do this even if we set off tomorrow morning from Toul to Rome by ourselves, with our staff and our boots and our vows. Our walk would not be his. I am sure that there are a number of people in the twentieth and twenty-first centuries who have or who will actually take Belloc's walk. They will have in their pocket his book as a guidebook. They will begin from Toul and end in Rome, even on the Feast of Sts. Peter and Paul. I envy them. They will try to eat and drink what he ate and drank where he ate and drank it. But "in divine Providence," as he calls it, this newer walk, for all its attention to place, weather, local characteristics, drawings, and scenery, will not see what Belloc saw. Belloc's book is an account of spirit, yes, of a spirit very much embodied in matter.

Belloc has no Manichean tendencies, of course, not even any Platonic tendencies that would see the whole man in his spirit or in his soul, though he does have a soul that connects him with *what is*.

> In early youth the soul can still remember its immortal habitation, and clouds and edges of hills are of another kind from ours, and every scent and colour has a savour of Paradise. . . . Youth came up that val-

ley of evening, borne upon a settled state, and their
now sudden influence upon the soul in short ecstasies
is the proof that they stand outside time, and are not
subject to decay. This, then, was the blessing of Sillano
[a small Italian town he had reached], and here was
perhaps the highest moment of those seven hundred
miles – or more (227).

The things that "stand outside of time," the things that can
be "had for nothing," the ability to recognize our "highest
moment" – such are the important things that make us
what we are, things that we might miss on our own walks
from Toul to Rome or wherever we might wander if we do
not first spend time with Belloc on his walk.

We know more about *The Path to Rome* if we realize
that in the following year, 1902, Belloc took another walk
in his native Sussex in England, where he intimates that
the original Garden of Eden was located. "The north is the
place for men. Eden was there, and the four rivers of
Paradise are the Seine, the Oise, the Thames, and the
Arun, there are grasses there, and the trees are generous,
and the air is an unnoticed pleasure" (242). What a
remarkable phrase – "an unnoticed pleasure!" We are such
earthlings that we think that we notice all our pleasures.
Belloc confesses that "I was not made for Tuscany."

This second 1902 walk, equally as charming as the 1901
Path to Rome, was called *The Four Men*. Needless to say,
each of the men on this latter excursion was Belloc himself.
I shall say something of this English walk in the conclusion
to this book. Suffice it to say here that both walks were
lonely affairs and therefore ironically both profound les-
sons in companionship. To know one another, indeed to
love one another, we also need silence, to be alone, the gift
of the contemplative tradition. Those who have no silence,
who do not sometimes walk alone, have no friends. Yet, *The
Path to Rome* is full of Belloc's affirmations that, after long
stretches by himself, he suddenly "has need of companionship."

II.

Belloc is often reviled for his famous sentence that "Europe is the faith and the faith is Europe." I cannot number the times that I have seen this sentence cited with horror and derision – and with much superficiality of understanding about what he meant by it. Yet, there is a truth to it that can be seen in this walk from Toul to Rome in the late spring and early summer of 1901, a walk that took Belloc over the Jura and the Alps in the snow, while traversing the plains of France and Italy in such heat that he mostly walked at night and slept by day wherever he could, sometimes in inexpensive inns, sometimes in a barn, often in the open under a tree or in the shade of bushes. He finds crosses and small chapels on the mountains. He sees the gentle hospitality of men in pubs and peasant women in serving him breakfast. He buys a good wine that sometimes tastes sour to him in the morning. We can feel his hunger and the delight of the fresh loaves that he finds in the little house that is the baker's, the one pointed out to him that has smoke coming out of the chimney early in the morning. Bakers, he thinks, are the finest of men because they have to arise so early and thus see the day come to be.

Belloc is adamantly "incarnational," that is, he does not separate the soul and the body. There is much in *The Path to Rome* about food and wine and sleep, as I have already intimated, almost as if it is all right to be the kind of beings we are. "It is quite clear that the body must be recognized and the soul kept in its place, since a little refreshing food and drink can do so much to make a man" (28). Belloc is always aware of the truth that Augustine knew that the great temptations, the great crimes, do not arise from the flesh but, as in the case of Lucifer himself, from the spirit. And even when they appear in the flesh, they usually, in some way obscure but reflectively traceable in us, are controlled by the spirit.

Yet, we too are beings with a certain sadness about us. There is ever a poignancy in every work of Belloc, even in his laughter and amusement, of which there is much. "Then let us love one another and laugh. Time passes, and we shall laugh no longer – and meanwhile common living is a burden, and earnest men are at siege upon us all around. Let us suffer absurdities, for that is only to suffer one another" (11). We are indeed under siege; what we believe in the faith of Europe is rejected more and more openly hence a hundred years from Belloc's walk. But we laugh. We are indeed absurdities. Suffering one another is not merely a suffering; it is also patience, a world full of laughter.

Early in his walk to Rome, to give a further example of his thinking on food, Belloc asks about breakfast. His very way of asking the question is delightful. "I would very much like to know what those who have an answer to everything can say about the food requisite to breakfast?" (31). "Those who have an answer for everything," we suspect, have, in Belloc's mind, few answers to anything. He recalls that Marlowe, Jonson, Shakespeare, and Spenser drank beer for breakfast plus a little bread. In his French regiment, he remembers, for breakfast they drank black coffee "without sugar," with a cut of a stale piece of bread to go with it.

The great (French) Republicans fought first and ate later. Belloc was also a sailor and ate "nothing for several hours." He continues:

> Dogs eat the first thing they come across, cats take a little milk, and gentlemen are accustomed to get up at nine and eat eggs, bacon, kidneys, ham, cold pheasant, toast, coffee, tea, scones, and honey, after which they will boast that their race is the hardiest in the world and ready to beat every fatigue in the pursuit of Empire. But what rule governs all of this? Why is breakfast different from all other things, so that the Greeks called it the best thing in the world. . . ? (32).

How amusing is this description of the breakfast of the hearty and hardy English gentleman, with its four meats plus eggs, in pursuit of Empire and oblivious of fatigue! And what was Greece if not a constant search for precisely "the best thing in the world?"

In re-reading *The Path to Rome*, what struck me was Belloc's sense that the authority of God was put into the world to unsettle us, that we could be here much too occupied with ourselves, that we really did not want to bother with revelation, especially if it meant any kind of revolution in our manners or in our morals.

> For when boys or soldiers or poets, or any other blossoms and prides of nature, are for lying steady in the shade and letting the Mind commune with its Immortal Comrades, up comes Authority busking about and eager as though it were a duty to force the said Mind to burrow and sweat in the matter of this very perishable world, its temporary habitation. "Up," says Authority, "and let me see that Mind of yours doing something practical. Let me see Him mixing painfully with circumstance, and botching up some Imperfection or other that shall at least be a Reality and not a silly Fantasy" (13).

These are profound, if diverting words. The temporary habitation of the mind can be quite pleasant to it. Why worry about anything else? It is best to lay "steady in the shade," to dream of worlds that perhaps might be, fantasies, to be sure. Authority is something of a pest. Yet, there are things to which Mind prefers not to pay attention, the first of which is Reality itself. How well does Belloc describe the men of our kind who are wont to favor their own musings over a more glorious reality that they could only receive, but not invent by themselves!

And yet, Belloc was prepared to do the things that men have done for thousands of years. His reasons for daily Mass are as profound as any seen in theological literature since. He gives four reasons. The first is "that for half-an-hour just at the opening of the day you are silent and recollected, and have to put off cares, interests, and passions in the repetition of a familiar action" (38–39). The second reason is ritual. "The function of all ritual (as we see in games, social arrangements, and so forth) [is] to relieve the mind of so much of responsibility and initiative and to catch you up (as it were) into itself, leading your life for you during the time it lasts" (39). The third reason is that you are inclined to good and reasonable thoughts; you are not distracted by that "busy wickedness" of self and others that is "the true source of human miseries." And finally, and most importantly, we do "what the human race has done for thousands upon thousands upon thousands of years. This is a matter of such moment that I am astonished people hear of it so little. Whatever is buried right into our blood from immemorial habit that we must be certain to do if we are to be fairly happy (of course no grown man or woman can really be very happy for long – but I mean reasonably happy). . . ." To do what our kind does, to realize that we have here no lasting city, that we can perhaps be "fairly happy," "reasonably happy" in this life, but to expect more is to reject the order of being and revelation in which we find ourselves.

III.

No doubt, the passage in *The Path to Rome* that I have most thought of over the years, the one that always strikes me anew when I read it again, occurs when Belloc is sitting in a Swiss town called Undervelier, by a stream, with a penny cigar. Recall that Belloc had an American wife from Napa, California. He had walked this country twice to see her. And to prove that he was not totally romantic about food, let me cite, at this odd point, the following delightful comparison: "They cook worse in Undervelier than any place I was ever in, with the possible exception of Omaha, Neb." (104). I might add, that I once had a very excellent supper with two of my cousins in precisely Omaha, Nebraska!

But bad food does not prevent Belloc from noticing that this mountain village of Undervelier contains believers who accept their faith almost naturally. He himself, he confesses, has not had this experience in his own life. For Belloc, faith was always "something fighting odds." He goes into the village church where he hears the congregation sing in a "Latin nearer German than French." They sing the Vespers hymn, *Te, lucis ante terminum*. He wonders about the nature of belief.

"Of its nature it breeds a reaction and an indifference" (102). This is again the problem of authority with which Belloc began his walk. Belloc notes that unbelievers and atheists, those who only "think and judge," cannot really understand the problem of Christians. For faith "of its nature struggles with us." In our youth we "inevitably reject it and set out in the sunlight content with natural things." Belloc, of course, is a born Catholic, that is, a man who is aware that we still have to come to terms with our faith even if we are baptized in our infancy. We think we can explain everything without it. We live our lives. To explain his point, he uses a mountain image. We are like men who go down the cleft of a mountain, things above are hidden by the rocks and cliffs. Suddenly, when we reach the bottom, "we look back and see our home."

We have not found anything better in "the natural things" wherein we look. We have once known a "home." So we return. Belloc asks about what causes this return? His answer is surprising: "I think it is the problem of living; for every day, every experience of evil, demands a solution." Our fantasies, our theories do not prove to be enough for us. We go on living, "every day." And we experience evil. It is not we, but "the experience of evil" that "demands a solution." And there is none to be found where we have been looking. We begin to remember at last "the great scheme." "Our childhood pierces through." In what must be an autobiographical note, Belloc tells us "that we who return [to the faith] suffer hard things; for there grows a gulf between us and many companions. We are perpetually thrust into minorities."

The world without faith talks "a strange language." And what is even worse, "we are troubled by the human machinery of a perfect and superhuman revelation; we are over-anxious for its safety, alarmed, and in danger of violent decisions." No doubt this observation is something that would be more pertinent to a Catholic, to a Church founded on Peter and the apostles. We forget that the human machinery is included in the superhuman revelation. We think we can save the world and the Church by ourselves. We cannot.

Belloc again travels on his way to Rome. "It is hard when a man has loved common views and is happy only with his fellows" (103). We have afresh the theme of why are we bothered with more than we can expect with just Mind? It is an "awful struggle" to reconcile two truths. We must not deny what "is certainly true" and yet we must keep "civic freedom sacred in spite of the organisation of religion." And in an astonishingly frank admission, Belloc writes, "it is hard to accept mysteries and to be humble." We must wrestle with faith and reason as "the great schoolmen were tost." Thus, faith, authority, that which is given to us just when we think we have everything figured out, annoys us, for it "leads us away, as by a command, from all that banquet of the intellect than which there is no keener joy known to man." Belloc is quite aware of unexpected pleasures, including the pleasure of intellect, its own delight in what it knows.

But Belloc has also accepted the mysteries. To be humble is difficult. "I went slowly up the village place in the dusk, thinking of this deplorable weakness of men that the Faith is too great for them, and accepting it as an inevitable burden. I continued to muse with my eyes upon the ground." We are, I suppose, wont to think of faith as a gift, which it is, and a joy, which it also is. But in Belloc we are aware of what it at stake, "this deplorable weakness of men that the Faith is too great for them." And of course, it is too great for them, that is why they are called to everlasting life, not just to sacred civic freedom.

The Path to Rome, in conclusion, is a charming, moving, unsettling book, mostly charming. It is a book that involves us in a walk of a century ago. We must take it some time. Belloc, at one point, sees the Lake of Bolsena in Italy from a high distance. He was in the south now – "I had become southern and took beauty for granted" (253). As he was sitting there, an old man in a pony cart came by. Belloc was tired. He again broke his vow about wheeled vehicles, though he does not attribute it to the temptation of the devil. As they raced down the hill, both sang. "I could not understand his songs nor he mine, but there was wine in common between us, and *salami*, and a merry heart, bread which is the bond of all mankind, and the prime solution of ill-ease – I mean the forgetfulness of money" (254). Bread is the bond of mankind and if we forget our money we will not be ill-at-ease.

So this is *The Path to Rome* which, if we are fortunate, we are fated to read more than a century after it was written, as Belloc himself intimated. As I said, there is ever a poignancy in Belloc. All good things "come to an end," as he tells us. This ending includes his book. Then in a passage of almost sublime beauty, he writes: "The leaves fall and they are renewed; the sun sets on the Vexin hills, but he rises again over the woods of Marly. Human companionship once broken can never be restored, and you and I shall not meet or understand each other again. It is so of all the poor links whereby we try to bridge the impassable gulf between soul and soul" (265).

Belloc then changes moods. He gives us the musical notes (I forgot to tell the reader about his wonderful sketches of the scenes he saw that are in the book). He sings: *"L'amore è una catena; l'amore è una catena; l'amore è una catena, Che non si spezza!"* – Love is a chain that is not broken. The impassable gulf between soul and soul, human companionship, the poor links – yet, as we read Belloc, as we walk with him in the valleys and hills, in the mountains and plains of Europe, we are left with a feeling that we did understand him, while we walked with him. The companionship can be taken up again more than a century later as we again read *The Path to Rome*.

Chapter II

WHAT DO PHILOSOPHERS KNOW?

"Reason must realize that human knowledge is a journey which allows no rest."

– John Paul II, Fides et Ratio, #18

"All men by nature desire to know. An indication of this is the delight we take in our senses; for even apart from their usefulness, they are loved for themselves; and above all others is the sense of sight. For not only with a view to action, but even when we are not going to do anything, we prefer seeing (one might say) to everything else. The reason is that this, most of all of the senses, makes us know and brings to light many differences between things."

– Aristotle, Metaphysics, Book I, Chapter 1, 980a23–28

"Truth is so obscure in these times, and falsehood so established, that unless we love the truth, we cannot know it."

– Pascal, (T1662), Pensées, #863

I.

What do philosophers do? In general, they try to reduce the disparate facts and principles found or observed in any walk of life or discipline to order. They see that contradictory principles cannot both be true. This mention of contradiction implies a reflective "examination" of the mind on itself about itself. We realize that we cannot "prove" the principle of contradiction, namely, that a thing cannot be and not be at the same time and in the same respect. It is where we begin if we are to begin at all. We cannot prove it from something "clearer," for nothing is more evident than the principle itself. We must assume the validity of the principle itself when we try to reject it. We cannot reject it without affirming it. The first exercise of intellectual freedom is the conscious, repeated effort to deny the principle of contradiction until finally we realize actively, in our own intellects, that it cannot be denied.

If it were true that contradictories could both be true in all circumstances, then anything can be true, including exact opposites. Likewise, the same things that are true would also, on the same grounds, be false. Thus, the principle of contradiction holds in its very denial or else the denial could not be valid. The mind presupposes this principle that comes into operative existence the moment we try to affirm or deny anything, once we know that something other than our mind exists. Indeed, we first know our own minds when we affirm or deny something that is not our mind. Our only alternative to examining or employing this principle, as Aristotle maintained, is to keep silence, to allow nothing to be examined or even spoken. But this "silence" would remove any rational being from any intercourse with other rational beings at any level. The denier of the principle would reduce himself to a vegetative state. We should, as Aristotle said in his *Rhetoric*, be more read to defend ourselves with our words than with our arms.

Robert Sokolowski, in a seminal essay, observed that what philosophers do is "make distinctions."[1] That is to say, they try to understand, to separate one thing from another, to relate things, to see what can and cannot go together. This very effort to make such distinctions is itself a delight, a fascination with things and our relation to them. Plato remarked in *The Republic* that the philosopher's function is to say of *what is*, that it is, and of what is not, that it is not. Notice that the philosopher affirms and denies, as if we need to make such a statement one way or another about the *things that are*. Indeed, making such statements is principally what the mind is for, its contemplative activity. This is what we mean by truth, the truth of things, which we desire to have even when we do not have it, even when we say it is "impossible," for that too, ironically, would be a "truth." We want to know whether what we affirm or deny in our minds does or does not conform with the way things are outside the mind.

Plato also tells us of the famous case of the Thracian maidens, who exemplify the ordinary person's view of the philosopher. Evidently, two famous philosophers were soberly walking down the road one day in Athens, speaking to each other of the things above, when one of them, not noticing a rather large pothole in the road, ignominiously fell in it. On witnessing this, to them, absurd, scene, these charming, normal young ladies are said to have "giggled." And this giggle has become immortal, for it suggests that philosophers, for all their hauteur, are highly impractical beings who can barely tie their shoestrings or notice holes in the road. What, after all, is the "use" of such impractical types that we have to lead around holes in the road so that they do not fall in them?

1 Robert Sokolowski, "The Method of Philosophy: Making Distinctions," *The Review of Metaphysics*, LI (March, 1998), 515–32.

II.

What do philosophers "do?" At bottom, they do nothing "useful." What they do is precisely, as Aristotle implied, "useless." However, nothing pejorative is intended when we observe the uselessness of the philosopher, provided we also understand that philosophers have been known to call truth "folly," as we read in St. Paul. Nothing prevents a philosopher from being a corrupt man whose intellectual system is not designed to know the truth but rather to protect his actions and deeds from any examination against the norms or standards of *what is*. Man, as Aristotle said, can be worse than the beasts, which comment, I have always thought, is a slander on the poor animals. In principle, those who are called to the highest of vocations are the same ones who can fall to the lowest. The examples of Lucifer in Scripture and of the tyrant in the classic authors are cases in point. Lucifer was the brightest of the angels. We can find little difference of raw talent between the philosopher-king and the worst tyrant, except in what each chooses, in what each calls his end, his "truth." Once the end, good or bad, is chosen, all prudence is designed to achieve it.

Pascal held that we must love the truth even to "know" it. Aristotle began his most rigorous book almost light-heartedly by telling us to delight in the things we see about us so that we could "make distinctions," which, if we think about it, we love to do. We love to know how things are alike and how they are different, and thus what they are, that they are. And philosophers can be lonely people. They can find themselves, as Daniel Mahoney pointed in his new book on *Solzhenitsyn*, in gulags with everything taken away from them and asked, in order to be "free," to affirm only one thing, namely, "a lie."[2] Plato said the same thing.

2 Daniel Mahoney, *Solzhenitsyn: The Ascent from Ideology* (Lanham, Md.: Rowman & Littlefield, 2001).

He told us that the worst thing we could have is a "lie" in our souls about the most important things. But surely he knew that a culture could also be filled with folks with such lies in their souls, not wanting to know and hence not choosing to follow the highest things.

What does a philosopher "know"? John Paul II, following a famous phrase in St. Augustine about our "restless hearts," told us that we are on a journey in the pursuit of knowledge that "allows us no rest." I love that phrase – "a journey that allows us no rest." The Pope is, of course, right. Some would have this comment mean that there is no "rest" ever. But this alternative, were it true, would just mean, as Aristotle also said, that we were the one being in the universe who is, as such, "in vain," to no purpose. Both reason and revelation exist in order that we know that our being, and with it the being of the cosmos, does not exist "in vain."

Still, what do philosophers know? Above all, they are supposed to "know themselves." However, to know oneself, we quickly realize, we must first know something that is not ourselves. To know ourselves, we must actually be knowing something not ourselves so that we are engaged in an act of knowing, an act the structure of which we do not give to ourselves but find it already there along with our being in which it exists. We can, on knowing something not ourselves, then reflect back on ourselves. We see that "what" is knowing what is not ourselves is indeed something we identify with the who and what we are.

But is it not rather dull, even vain, to know ourselves? Of course, we soon discover that we are unlike any other being in the universe. We ought to know this uniqueness about ourselves, as it corresponds to the truth of our being. The peculiar thing about our knowing is that we begin with an empty slate, as Aristotle put it. If we know nothing or everything, we have the same mind, the same capacity to know. In one case it is, as it were, filled; in the other case, it is empty. It is not a perfection of the mind to know nothing. And since we are not gods, since we are finite, we know after our own manner of knowing, though we really do know some things.

Yet, even when we know and know that we know something, we remain "restless." Is this a bad thing? It is a bad thing only if we do not first delight in *what is*, in what is not ourselves that is out there, as it were, for us to know. Our minds are in fact *capax omnium*, capable of knowing all things. The fact that we do not yet know all things is merely the other side of the journey on which we are engaged by our very living and, indeed, dying. Some, I know, despair because they do not yet know everything. But this not-yet-knowing is not a cause of despair. Again the regulating principle is that of Aristotle, of delighting not merely in seeing, but also in knowing, knowing anything, but especially in knowing the order of things. And to know the order of things, we must make distinctions, to say that this is, but this is not that.

III.

What do philosophers know? One of the things they know, perhaps the most important thing they know, is that they have questions that are not answered, even when some questions are answered. They assume that their answers will also come from philosophy, but this is an assumption, though not an entirely wrong one. Yet, if they do not have the questions of our being properly formulated, they will not know whether answers are proposed to their questions as asked. Nothing requires that answers be given to people who ask no questions, or who ask improperly formulated questions.

Should we worry that philosophers do not see answers? Should we worry that some philosophers are corrupt as philosophers, that is, that they refuse to go in one or another direction because they see, at least darkly, where reality might lead them but they do not want to go there, do not want to change their lives? Indeed, we should worry about these things. Philosophers know that they must ask, "why there is something, not nothing?" "Why is this thing not that thing?" They know that a thing cannot be and not be at the same time in the same respect. They know they have intellectual tools. They know that their philosophical knowledge, as such, does not change the world, but it does change them. They are more when they know that *what is*, is, and what is not, is not.

What do philosophers know? This is my last comment. Philosophers know the delight of knowing what is not themselves. This is what they speak to their friends about, what they want to do above all. Philosophy, when done well, when done rightly, leaves us in a state of expectancy, of wanting no rest, not because we are tired, but because there is so much yet to see, yes so much to see again and again. We did not make reality; it is given to us. This too is a truth of philosophy.

In the end, the "private" lives of our kind and the public events in our world both cause us to wonder. Wondering about such common events, the things that need order, as Aristotle implied, is still the beginning of philosophy. But the end of philosophy is the knowing, the delight in affirming of *what is* that it is, and of what is not, that it is not.

Chapter III

THE PROBLEM OF PHILOSOPHIC LEARNING

"Visitor from Elea: 'But if an important issue needs to be worked out well, then as everyone has long thought, you need to practice on unimportant, easier issues first. So that's my advice to us now, Theaetetus, since we think it's hard to hunt down and deal with the kind, sophist, we ought to practice our method of hunting on something easier first – unless you can tell us about another way that's somehow more promising.'

"Theaetetus: 'I can't.'"

– *Plato*, The Sophist, *218cd*

"From the first I regarded Oxford as a place to be inhabited and enjoyed for itself, not as the preparation for anywhere else. . . . At Oxford I was reborn in full youth. My absurdities were those of exuberance and naivety, not of spurious sophistication. I wanted to do everything and know everyone, [but] not with any ambition to insinuate myself into fashionable London or make influential friends who should prosper any future career. . . . My interests were as narrow as the ancient walls. I wanted to taste everything

Oxford could offer and consume as much as I could hold."

   – Evelyn Waugh, A Little Learning.[1]

"No spontaneous operation of intellectual relations protects the young philosopher against the risk of delivering his soul to error by choosing his teachers infelicitously."

   – Yves Simon, A General Theory of Authority[2]

I.

The perfect breakfast, it seems to me, is a freshly baked, genuine butter croissant with a cup of coffee or chocolate. But the *perfect* croissant is hard to come by, at least if we are not in France where it seems miraculously to reappear every morning. We have croissants at breakfast where I live. They are rather smallish, not very flaky, generally doughy, flat-tasting, though certainly not inedible. I have kept my eye open for the perfect croissant. Walter Kerr once said that we should never eat "bad" ice cream. We may have to eat bad bread, or even dried-out croissants, to stay alive. But ice cream and croissants are eaten primarily because they are tasty and delicious. There is nothing sybaritic or epicurean about this truth. It is simply an acknowledgment of the being of a thing.

We do not "need" either ice cream or croissants, yet the things we do not "need" are often symbolic of the best part of our nature. Leon Kass, in his book, *The Hungry Soul: Eating and the Perfection of Our Nature,* has spelled this principle out with some elegance.[3] We are not only beings who feed or eat, but beings who dine together. Our bodies

---

1 Evelyn Waugh, *A Little Learning* (Boston: Little Brown, 1964), 171.
2 Yves Simon, *A General Theory of Authority* (Notre Dame, Ind.: University of Notre Dame Press, 1980), 100.
3 Leon Kass, *The Hungry Soul: Eating and the Perfection of Our Nature* (Chicago: University of Chicago Press, 1994).

and lives are so attuned that they respond to our inner soul. We can make matter tasty, beautiful. And this making is perhaps our highest vocation in this world, as Plato taught us, when something *that is*, by being *what it is*, leads us to what is beautiful.

At the beginning of the Second Book of *The Republic*, we find a famous conversation between Socrates, Glaucon, and his brother Adeimantus about the praise of justice for its own sake. The two young men, Plato's brothers, are highly commended by Socrates for being able to state the case against justice so well, but still they were not convinced by it. Thus they wanted to listen to the philosopher explain why a worthy life was a good even if one suffered for it or even if no reward resulted from it. What interests me here are the reasons that young Glaucon gives to Socrates about how he sees the need for what I call "philosophic learning."

Glaucon begins the conversation: "Tell me, do you think there is a kind of good we welcome, not because we desire what comes from it, but because we welcome it for its own sake – joy, for example, and all the harmless pleasures that have no results beyond the joy of having them?" Socrates acknowledges the existence of such things. And Glaucon continues, "And is there a kind of good we like for its own sake and also for the sake of what comes from it – knowing, for example, and seeing and being healthy?" (357b–c). Joy, we note, is something for its own sake. There are indeed "pleasures that have no results beyond the joy of having them." And joy is what we possess when we have what we love, when what we love is *what is* and its cause.

Several years ago, down on "N" Street just before Wisconsin Avenue in Washington, to continue this analogy, there was a small patisserie called *"Au Croissant Chaud."* After some shopping around, I decided that the croissants at this little shop proved to be not only the best in Washington, but, surprisingly, the cheapest. The shop had tables outside in a pleasant patio on which to eat them in leisure. Even on a cold morning, it was worth doing. The patisserie was run by a family, either Spanish or French speaking, I never was quite sure. I was a frequent patron. The place was to croissants what the National Gallery is to art.

Much to my chagrin, one morning this shop closed. I shopped around subsequently for several years for the perfect croissant. As I have intimated, there is really not much sense in eating a croissant unless it is very good, though one should be careful of demanding such perfection that he misses in this life the fact that *what is*, is good, even if not perfect. The search for perfection does not necessarily exclude the less than perfect, a principle, if we think of it, that is the very charter of our own being in this world, of the possibility that we too in experiencing joy and delight begin to have intimations of *what is*, of what exists in light and radiance.

I tried the other French bakeries with the same unhappy results, though again I ate them. In fact, I have been somewhat frustrated with the saga of less than great croissants. I begin to wonder if there is not revealed here a deeper problem of soul than we might at first sight realize. In seeking the *perfect* croissant, a worthy enterprise as it seems to me, I wonder what indeed am I looking for in all that I do? It is a question that ought to arise in the pursuit of any real good, I think, including the perfect croissant.

On campus not too long ago, I came across a young French girl who is in one of my classes. She was carrying a cake box. She told me that she found a new French patisserie on Wisconsin and Q Streets called *Café Poupon*. I had never noticed it. Evidently, they put up unsold cakes for sale at half-price at four PM every day. Naturally, a couple of days later, I hastened with great eagerness over to sample the product. Much to my delight, the lady behind the counter was the very one who used to run the old *Au*

Croissant Chaud. However, the croissant I sampled was not just perfect. My heart was both delighted to find this place with real croissants and broken that what I ate was not the best.

Why am I beginning these thoughts on "philosophical learning" with this tale of my search for the "perfect croissant"? It is a very Platonic enterprise, of course. In the *Gorgias*, Plato conveniently compares oratory to the product of pastry chefs, by extension to the baker of croissants. Plato is troubled that elegance of language or taste can deflect us from the truth or the cause of what is beautiful. We can indeed separate pleasure from the reality in which it exists and gives it its purpose. Yet, we know, that Socrates himself was the greatest of orators who sought to persuade us daily to seek what is good, what is beautiful, through the *things that are*. To find things that are "perfect," it seems, we must begin with things less than perfect. Socrates is sometimes accused of being so absorbed by the perfect, by the best, that he shows a certain contempt for ordinary changing realities. But I think this accusation is not a correct reading of Socrates. Even in learning, he tells us, in *The Sophist*, to begin with easier things.

II.

Socrates always denied that he was a "teacher," however much the fathers of Charmides and Theages in the dialogues named after them begged him to take charge of their sons, to teach them how to live. But if even Socrates, the philosopher, did not teach, from whom do we learn? Surely, he did not mean that there were no teachers, and if no teachers, no students, though this is what he implies in the *Meno*. The subject that I want to propose here is precisely that of "philosophic learning," learning about the highest things, learning about the whole of *what* is. Surely nothing can be more important than such learning, whatever else is important. Learning is not merely a question of truth. It is also a question of choosing the truth when we begin to know it. Knowledge is, as Socrates said, one of those things that both cause joy and delight for its own sake but is also useful for other things.

There is a paradox here of more than passing significance. For it is possible for us to deny that the good is good or the beautiful is beautiful, even when it stands before us. Part of the reason we can make this denial is because what is finitely beautiful is not beauty itself, even when it is really beautiful. Even the *perfect* croissant points beyond itself, unsettles us. It too should be eaten and enjoyed, not just preserved in some bakery museum. The other reason that we can deny what is good or beautiful even when it is before us in its splendor is that we can still manage to direct our souls, our attention to some other lesser good or beauty. We can absorb ourselves in particular goods, real goods. We can refuse to examine ourselves. The "unexamined life (that) is not worth living," to cite a famous phrase of Socrates in *The Apology*, can make us content with some real but disordered good that will eventually corrupt our souls because we choose not to follow to its end the finite beauty that initially attracts us. As Aristotle shows us in the First Book of his *Ethics*, all the definitions of good that we come up with in our pursuit of happiness have real worth. Ironically, we can do nothing wrong unless we also at the same time do something right, but something "right" out of order. We fail to put something in the good that ought to be there. Evil is the "lack" of a good that ought to be there – as the famous definition goes.

What I want to suggest is that if we choose not to learn what is fundamental, we will indeed not learn it. Or, to put it another way, we can choose as our end, as our definition of happiness as it applies to us and defines all we deliberate and decide upon, something that will betray the best in us. As Aristotle put it, if we choose as our end anything but contemplation, anything but knowledge of *what* is, for its own sake, we will fail not merely ourselves, but one another. Indeed, we will misjudge our place in the cosmos as precisely the *microcosmoi*, the beings in whom something of everything exists. We are not gods. Nor are we beasts. We are precisely the mortals, the finite beings who need not exist, but nonetheless who do exist and who do act following our own particular kind of existence. When we choose what is good, we are the best of the animals; when we choose badly, we are the worst, again to recall Aristotle.

One of the charges directed against Socrates was that he "corrupted the youth." He denied it. The youth who listened to him did so of their own accord, as a kind of amusement. Socrates, unlike modern professors, never took money for anything, especially teaching. The Sophists did receive fees for teaching whether what was taught was true or not. For this effort, they are sometimes called the first university professors, the first humanists. The compliment is enigmatic. Aristotle tells us not to listen to those intellectuals who, being human, tell us to listen to only human and mortal things. What is true is simply free. It can bear no cost. Truth as such cannot be patented or copyrighted. Our highest conversations thus are not only free but of things we have in common, of things whose origin is not ourselves, even though directed to our minds that we might know them. No wonder Plato says that when we first come to know something, our immediate instinct is to hurry out to tell someone of it.

Moreover, Socrates humbly claimed that he only knew what he did not know, even though the "old accusers" at the beginning of *The Apology* charged that he made the weaker argument seem stronger. The philosopher, no doubt, perplexes the non-philosopher. The non-philosopher wants to drive him out of the city or to keep him strictly private. The philosopher, when too proud, moreover, is tempted to see this common man's perplexity as a sign of his own success, his own power. But it is not so. Vision and clarity are his calling. The pure of heart will see God. The blind cannot lead the blind. The philosopher is not at home in existing cities even when he must live in them. But without him, cities know only themselves. They exclude the high culture that asks whether what they are is what they ought to be. The high culture, the city in speech, transcends all existing cities and judges them, without repudiating their need. This is the high vocation of philosophic learning, to plant the city in speech in each of our souls so that we can be free of what is not true, of what is not good. This vocation can happen even in the worst regime, where evil must be mostly suffered. It can be ignored in the best regime, where pleasure is separated from that in which it exists in order.

The youth who were said to be corrupted by Socrates' activities in Athens were not his pupils. They listened to him in the streets, to be sure, but mostly as a form of afternoon entertainment. They had nothing better to do. They were escaping the discipline of their families. They delighted in what was odd or infamous or provoking, whatever it was. Socrates, talking to important Athenians in pursuit of his Delphic vocation to know himself, was the best show in town. The sons went home after listening to Socrates examine their fathers, the businessman, the poet, and the lawyer.

The sons were eager to imitate the philosopher. They tried out their new-fangled skills on their fathers, the rulers of the city. This second-hand philosophy only infuriated the fathers and incited them against Socrates as one who corrupts the youth and, through them, the city. The youth who followed Socrates, if any did, undermined the existing city. It was probably this domestic fury between father and son, more than anything else, that was responsible for Socrates' legal death, a death that posed, and still poses, the problem of truth to the city that does not like to hear it. Thus, Socrates chose to live privately, as long as he could. He knew he was not safe among those who held power but not truth. He also hoped that some who heard him would carry on his teaching because the fathers would kill the philosopher but not the sons.

III.

In one sense, no doubt, Socrates did "corrupt" the youth, if the effort to learn the truth can be called a "corruption," which it can be in a city founded on wants or passions. Socrates calls his city a "noble lie" because all who hear of it, besides the philosopher himself, will think it untrue. He followed his divine vocation to examine whether he was indeed, as the Oracle said, the wisest man in Greece, something he at first doubted. But, in the process, he revealed that the pillars of the *polis*, the poet, the lawyer, and the craftsman, did not know more than their own narrow specialties. The existing city could not, however, be passed on in the same form to the next generation if it lost confidence in the city's own actual founding, a founding that differed from the principles of the city in speech. This doubting of the city's worth was the effect of Socrates' example. He founded another city that must be founded again and again in the souls of potential philosophers. The careful reading of Plato is the beginning of this new founding in any existing city. An education that does not end here, in the city in speech, is not worth having.

Socrates' way of life made him appear odd, un-civic. He seemed like a fool or a madman. Existing cities, especially democracies, were always considerably less than perfect. They were the best of the worst regimes. They were also places of danger to the philosopher. To be sure, in a regime of unprincipled liberty, such as Athens, it was difficult, as I said, to tell the difference between a fool and a philosopher. The philosopher seemed silly, eccentric, crazy. Democratic freedom meant that there were no common principles of distinction. Liberty meant doing what one wanted, not what was right. Right and wrong had no objective distinction. Both fool and philosopher seemed equally quaint in the existing city since there was no standard or measure by which we could distinguish them one from another. In a disordered regime, the good man is abnormal; the fool seems wise. This is why democrats prefer what is average, even what is bizarre, to what is true. The fluctuating average becomes the norm of truth. Much evil is justified on the grounds that everyone lies, cheats, steals. This is the teaching of Machiavelli, a teaching already recognized as a corruption in the First Book of *The Republic*.

Socrates was safe in Athens only if he remained a private citizen. But because he was imitated by the youth, the potential philosophers, he was forced against his wishes into court, a setting unfamiliar to him, as he told the jurors of Athens. On the day before his trial, he had tried to escape from the poet Meletus's' charge of impiety by attempting to learn from Euthyphro how to be pious. But Euthyphro, who was himself impiously trying in the courts his own father for murder, did not seem either to know what piety was or how to teach it. When on the next day, the poet Meletus led the court against him, Socrates could honestly claim that he tried to learn what piety was in order to reject the claim that he was impious. Thus, Socrates was accused of impiety, of being an atheist, of not believing in the gods of the city. In a very sophisticated argument, he denied the accusation. He believed in spirit. He knew where philosophy led, beyond matter, to immortality of the soul, to *what is*.

But Socrates' philosophy did lead him to oppose some of the accounts in Homer and Hesiod about the scandalous deeds of some of the gods of Athens. The educator of Greece corrupted its youth when they read its noblest, most enchanting literature. Thus, if Homer charmed us who did not yet know the philosophic life, the most famous student of Socrates would have to find a way to charm us even more than Homer in order to counteract the effects of the poetry that educated Greece. This same poetry also corrupted it, Socrates thought. We must find a city in speech and reproduce it in our own souls if we are to find a charm beyond that of Homer, whose charm not even Socrates denied.

The problem of "philosophic learning," as I call it, begins with our awareness that, to be ourselves, we are being called by something beyond ourselves. This is, as it were, the problem of the "perfect croissant" on the human level. And our capacity to be called out of ourselves begins with our sudden realization that we cannot fully explain ourselves to ourselves. The careful reading of the account of the young Plato on the death of his mentor is the first step in our effort to find a source that would explain ourselves when we are in some sense an enigma to ourselves. In any university, the reading of Plato is also a judge of that same university. Indeed, unless there is a reading of Plato, there is no university, and it is best to escape from any institution that does not know this, does not live by it. In spite of what he sometimes implies, Plato was also a poet. His charm, his oratory, call us out of existing cities, out of existing academies.

IV.

On September 11, 2000, John Paul II received in audience in Rome the rector, faculty, and students of the Jagiellonian University in Kraków, his beloved school. In his address to these Polish compatriots, the Pope recalled the words he used in his visit to Kraków in 1997. "The duty of an academic institution," the Holy Father, himself a master teacher, told his Polish friends, "is in a certain sense to give birth to souls for the sake of knowledge and wisdom, to shape minds and hearts. The task cannot be achieved other than through a generous service to the truth – revealing it and passing it on to others."[4] Academic

4 *L'Osservatore Romano* (October 4, 2000), 9.

institutions have their duties, purpose. There are things to be passed on.

In this brief passage, we catch the words of Plato – to give birth in souls. We catch the spirit of Pascal that knowledge includes the heart. We are reminded that truth is the object or purpose of intellect. And we even see the words of St. Thomas, the *contemplata tradere*, that truth is to be pondered first in our own souls and then to be passed on to others. What is first contemplated is to be passed on. But we must first experience the joy of knowing itself in our own souls. If we ever have the exhilarating experience of truth in our souls, we cannot but seek to tell others of it, to pass it on.

We are not first to read these words in terms of "obligation," though we cannot but be mindful of the end of the Gospels that command a going forth and a teaching of all nations. There is a superabundance to truth as to being. The first reaction we have to truth is simply a delight that *what is*, is. As Plato said, that truth is to say of *what is*, that it is, and of what is not, that it is not. The second reaction to truth is, as I have noted, the almost irresistible desire to tell someone else of it. It wants to flow out of us. It assumes that others seek it, that we belong to a kind that seeks to know. It implies that there is something into which we are all taken up, secured, made worthy.

The French historian Régine Pernoud recounts, with some amusement, a conference of French intellectuals devoted to the topic, "Were the Middle Ages Civilized?" She noted that this question seems to have been asked with little sense of humor or irony. These academics seemed incapable of seeing their own blindness. "The discussion ([on the Middle Ages] took place in Paris, on the rue Madame," Pernoud recalls. "One hopes," she added,

> for the moral comfort of the participants, that none of them, in order to return to his residence, had to pass

by Notre-Dame de Paris. He might have felt a certain uneasiness. But no, let us reassure ourselves: an employed academic is, in any case, physically incapable of seeing what is not in conformity with the notions his brains exudes. Thus he would not in any way have seen Notre-Dame, even if his path took him to the Place du Parvis.[5]

Even though I am, to use Pernoud's ironic phrase, "an employed academic," albeit with a vow of poverty, her words get to the heart of what I want to emphasize here, namely the peculiar blindness by which we do not see what is in fact there. We can actually walk in front of Notre Dame and wonder if the Middle Ages, which built Notre Dame, were civilized! The real question is whether we, with our question, are civilized? And most often, as Aristotle also had observed, the reason we do not see things, the reason we are blind to *what is*, is largely caused by our own theories, by our own choices on how we live.

What is at stake, we might ask ourselves, in the privilege of attending a university in our youth? Callicles, the smooth, dangerous politician in Plato's *Gorgias*, said that he even enjoyed studying philosophy in college, but, for heaven's sake, we put it away when we reach political power that cannot be impeded by philosophic musings with young scholars. Evelyn Waugh's autobiography was aptly entitled *A Little Learning*, a title intended, without saying so, to recall from Alexander Pope, that "little learning is a dangerous thing."[6] Actually, "much learning" can be an even more dangerous thing. We already recalled how the little learning of the potential philosophers about Socrates led him into considerable danger. Waugh himself was

5 Régine Pernoud, *Those Terrible Middle Ages* (San Francisco: Ignatius Press, 2000), 12.
6 Evelyn Waugh, *A Little Learning* (Boston: Little, Brown, 1964).

delighted at his arrival at Oxford. He wanted to enjoy it for its own sake; he wanted to "do" everything, to "know" everything, yes, to "taste" everything. Yet, to do such things well, indeed to do them at all, we need to be taught. Not all philosophers are worthy. Any city knows that at the origins of its public disorders we find primarily the disordered souls of its own teachers and philosophers.

But it is not the job of the politician to confute the philosopher whose own soul is disordered, though it is his task to use his common sense to protect the citizens from the aberrations of the philosophers. Simon's warning that nothing can protect the potential philosopher from giving himself to an errant academic is well taken. We are not to forget the primal vice of pride and how it relates to the most intelligent of the angels. The ultimate difference between the philosopher and the tyrant is not that one is more intelligent than the other. Rather it has to do with what good the one or the other chooses. And the root of all sin and disorder is the choice of oneself as the cause of being, as the cause of all the moral and intellectual distinctions. These are, I think, sobering words that do not allow us to be naive about our lot, about the drama into which we are born, about the city in which we live, especially if we do not also know of the city in speech, the *Civitas Dei*, that orders our souls.

Aristotle speaks in *The Ethics* of what happens when a politician is wholly absorbed in politics. He knows nothing of the pleasures of learning, of philosophy, so that, in its spiritual emptiness, his own soul turns to the passions and pleasures of the world. We are wont to admit that politics is a full-time occupation, a wholly absorbing profession. But it is a dangerous one, as Plato has often reminded us, when it is the only occupation we have, when we have only the existing city, not the city in speech, in our souls. The problem of "philosophical learning" lies here, I think.

V.

In Western literature we find a theme that associates life and drama. Indeed, it is often the drama that enables us to see or appreciate what life is about. In its ordinariness, we may easily fail to see the drama of life. This is why it is said that we truly live at a higher level when we contemplate life at a drama. This is a theme from Plato himself. Allan Bloom put it this way in his *Shakespeare's Politics*: "What is essentially human is revealed in the extreme, and we understand ourselves better through what we might be. In a way, the spectators live more truly when they are watching a Shakespearean play than in their daily lives, which are so much determined by the accidents of time and place."[7] It is the opportunity to live "more truly" that defines us perhaps more than anything else, even when all lives have their worthiness.

When Sally was about one year old, her mother ordered Charlie Brown to walk her around the neighborhood in a stroller. As a result of his reluctant obedience, Charlie could not manage the baseball team. When he walked Sally over near the game, the team shouted out at him for abandoning them. They were quite annoyed. Sally, who was just beginning to talk, was taking this all in. She was a problem. Finally, near the end of the game, when the team still had a chance to win if Charlie could pinch hit, he decides to rush Sally back home, grab his glove and bat and return as a hero to save the team. He tells a perplexed Sally, "I'm sorry I can't push you any more Sally but I have to go save the team from defeat." We see him in the next scene rushing back to the field yelling, "Hang on, Team! Here comes your faithful manager!" The last scene shows baby Sally near her front steps pondering the mystery of why she, at one year old, has caused so many problems. She says to herself, "I had no idea that life would be filled

---

7 Allan Bloom, *Shakespeare's Politics* (Chicago: University of Chicago Press, 1964), 9.

with such drama!" This is the real point of our human lot, is it not? We really have no idea of the drama of our existence in time. Needless to say, when Charlie got back to the field and to the plate, he struck out, much to the derision of the very team his disobedience was trying to save.[8]

We have no idea that our lives could be filled with such drama. Just because we seek the highest things, it does not follow that we do not pursue and enjoy other things. Aristotle had it about right: "Whatever someone regards as his being, or the end for which he chooses to be alive, that is the activity he wishes to pursue in his friend's company. Hence some friends drink together, others play dice, while others do gymnastics and go hunting, or do philosophy. They spend their days together on whichever pursuit in life they like most, for since they want to live with their friends, they share the actions in which they find the common life" (1172a2–7). Some do philosophy together.

What, in conclusion, would be the worst thing we could imagine for ourselves? Socrates asks Adeimantus "Don't you know that a *true* falsehood, if one may call it that, is hated by all gods and humans?" Adeimantus wonders what this might mean. "I mean that no one is willing to tell falsehoods to the most important part of himself about the most important things, but of all places he is the most afraid to have falsehood there." Adeimantus still does not quite get it. "That is because you think I'm saying something deep," Socrates replies. "I simply mean that to be false to one's soul about the things that are, to be ignorant and to have and hold falsehood here, is what everyone would least of all accept, for everyone hates a falsehood in that place most of all" (382a–b).

Plato often ends things with a prayer. Let me cite the one at the end of the *Phaedrus*: "O dear Pan and all the other gods of this place, grant that I may be beautiful

8 Charles Schulz, *Let's Face It, Charlie Brown* (New York: Fawcett, 1959).

inside. Let all my external possessions be in friendly harmony with what is within. May I consider the wise man rich. As for gold, let me have as much as a moderate man could bear and carry with him" (279c). This is where the pursuit of the perfect croissant leads, to a philosophic learning that, having inspired and guided us to be beautiful inside, incites us to make all things as beautiful as the being they bear allows.

All beauty is unsettling. We have, because of it, "restless hearts," as that great African lover of Plato told us (*Confessions*, I, 1). In the *Laws*, the Athenian stranger tells us that the purpose of war is peace and order. The wise man is rich. None of us knew in advance that life could be filled with such drama. No one is willing to tell falsehoods to the most important part of himself about the most important things. Yet, the Sophists tell us that they can teach us whatever we want to know, whether good or bad, without themselves being good or bad. Some friends drink together, others play dice, do gymnastics, go hunting. Still others do philosophy. Callicles said that we should put philosophy aside when we are young because politics is too serious for such adult playing. Socrates, the philosopher, was killed by Athens, the democracy, in 399 bc. The problem of philosophic learning abides in our souls only if we build a city in speech there, where we do not want to lie to ourselves about *what is*.

On finishing the main argument of this reflection, I was in a dental office in Chevy Chase, waiting to have a tooth filled. I looked at a magazines called *Biography*. Not much there but an article on F. Scott Fitzgerald. I next picked up the October 2000 issue of *Gourmet*, which someone had just put down. In thumbing through the pages, what do I see but an article on "great croissants," how to tell them, how to make them. After I explained my interest, the lady in the dental office kindly gave me this magazine. In it I read, "Delicately crisp outside, light yet chewy inside, enough sugar to accentuate the butter's sweetness, and enough salt to balance that sweetness. In a word, perfect" (224). Exactly. But the distance between the reading and the eating is infinite. The perfect croissant, the so much drama in life, Oxford as a place to be enjoyed for itself, not choosing our teachers infelicitously, no falsehood in the most important place in our souls, the prayer of Pan that we may be beautiful inside – such are the main steps in philosophical learning, in the discovery of *all that is*.

Chapter IV

THE ALTERNATIVE WORLD

"The root cause of sin, of falling away from God and from goodness and toward evil, is man's prideful self-centeredness. He attempts – although unsuccessfully – to ignore his Creator and his Ruler and to set up himself, his own will, as the hub of the universe. Refusing to acknowledge his lacks and limitations as a creature, he tries to upset the whole order of the universe by his perverse imitations of God."

– Herbert Deane, The Political and Social Ideas of St. Augustine, *1963*[1]

I.

An friend of mine was recently explaining to high school students what Catholics in particular might expect in the future from our secularist society. "You need not worry," she confidently told them, "that you will be stoned like St. Stephen or beheaded like St. Thomas More. But you can expect to be ridiculed and probably denied jobs or social acceptance if you actually practice your faith." After the talk, a young girl came up to my friend. She disagreed with

---

1 Herbert A. Deane, *The Political and Social Ideas of St. Augustine* (New York: Columbia University Press, 1963), 17.

this analysis. Already on her campus, the student told her, she has been "spat upon just for being what she is."

We do know of the astonishingly large number of martyrs in our time.[2] We also know of the relative indifference the supposedly distant persecution of Christians has aroused throughout the world, even among Christians themselves. The main thing to remember is that "religious fanatics" are now seen to be the main cause preventing the remaining elements of the complete secularization of man from being legally put into place. There is a real hatred of man as he is pictured in natural law and in the Gospels. Marx thought that religion was dangerous to man because it deflected his attention to the transcendent away from this worldly occupations. Today, religion and philosophy are dangerous simply because of what they are and hold.

Orthodox Catholics are naive to think they are not already included in the category of "religious fanaticism," along with Muslim, Orthodox Jewish, and other forms of religious awareness that something is radically wrong with the modern state and its supporting culture. "Inculturation," that oft-heard word, from now on will demand the souls of Christians to embrace the dogmatic secular culture. The one culture into which we dare not "inculturate" ourselves is the culture that finds nothing in human nature or society except what man put there by his own will and choice. Within the Church, moreover, already large numbers have accepted the essential doctrines of secularism and work to transform doctrine and practice to something malleable, able to conform to the principles of the secular order. Such Christians have reinterpreted Christianity to conform to modernity's tenets. These latter will not, so they think, be persecuted.

The problem of the modern world has long been how to silence Socrates without the nasty business of killing him,

2 See Robert Royal, *Catholic Martyrs of the Twentieth Century* (New York: Crossroads, 2000).

or how to tame the teachings of Christ without putting Him on the Cross. Both Socrates and Christ, when taken seriously, however, ask us to examine our lives, to be converted. That is, neither could be what he was without asking us to analyze the way we live, without implying that some relation exists between how we think and how we live, that there are wrong and right ways of living. What Paul told the Galatians is today very "anti-multicultural," to coin a phrase, very revolutionary, if not shocking. These are his words: "Now the works of the flesh are plain: immorality, impurity, licentiousness, idolatry, sorcery, enmity, strife, jealousy, anger, selfishness, dissension, party spirit, envy, drunkenness, carousing, and the like. I warn you . . . that those who do such things shall not inherit the kingdom of God" (5, 19–20). We do not want to hear such things even spoken among us.

Many of the things on Paul's list of aberrations have become "rights" and are featured activities in the media and other high places. Practitioners may not inherit the "kingdom of God" (though we dare not suggest that anyone, no matter what he does or holds, is not "saved"), but they do find honorable places in the land. Few, if any, items of Paul's enumeration are considered threats to any public order. They have no status outside wholly private opinion, if then. To do one or its opposite is equally acceptable to the public good. Civil society can be indifferent to them, except perhaps when they cause public messiness, which by definition is not the result in anything "wrong" in the action itself. It is merely an unfortunate crossing of equally legitimate desires and ways of life.

We believe in tolerance for all but the intolerant, that is to say, for those who suggest some things are wrong, objectively wrong. Intolerance has come to be defined as objecting in any way to any "value" that someone may freely embrace. This position presents no small problem because Christians are told, from their own resources, to "go forth and teach all nations," while at least some people still listen to Socrates long enough to suspect that, if he is right, something is very wrong with us. The theory of neutrality invariably embraces a contradiction, something in principle unthinkable. Aristotle says our whole moral and political lives ought to consist in praising and blaming what ought to be praised and blamed. The law, in the pursuit of its neutrality, cannot be neutral. It must take sides even while maintaining that there are no sides that make any difference. To make what is wrong to be "neutral" is already to take the first step in the long process of declaring what is wrong to be in fact right. Without a valid theory of natural law, it is exceedingly difficult to imagine how something we have a legal "right" to is not morally right.

For a while, we believed that we could solve our problems with the distinction between private and public, even though both Plato and Paul intimated that the public problems come from the private ones. Religion, philosophy, and morals would thus be "private" things. Hobbes, indeed, removed religious and philosophic discussions from the state by threat of force because they caused strife and did not have anything to do, he thought, with the external order. Public peace would simply be defined and enforced as what the state wanted. Provided we could accept the idea that ideas and beliefs made no difference, this solution was the epitome of simplicity. Civil force cured religious and philosophic fanaticism. It also denied us the possibility of distinguishing between good and bad states except on the principle of a peace due to imposed order that denied any importance to higher things.

The modern public order thus conceived itself to be neutral or minimalist, allowing the important things to be handled on voluntary bases. The "temporal common good" would not need or depend on rightness of soul or proper definition of virtue and vice. The distinctions of virtue and vice, like the definitions of happiness, would be totally private. We would have a "value-free" public life because we have a value-free private life. No objective or natural order existed according to which some distinction of right and wrong could be ascertained apart from our subjective preferences, even these differed from person to person. The state would be benevolent, something designed to aid us to achieve our "values" and "rights," no matter what they were. The only restriction would be of the intolerant who wanted to suggest that not all values or rights were harmless. If someone has a "right" to be a practicing homosexual of whatever sort, then the sickness or death that this activity might cause in the public order becomes the obligation of the state to remove, not of the individual to avoid the causes. The neutral state acquires the "duty" to make the "right" possible and safe. The state allows the "right" to bear whatever content it wants, including marriage and children, however they come to be. Objecting to this on moral or scientific grounds is "fanaticism" and therefore intolerant. The only order is the enforced order.

II.

The logic of our situation is fascinating. We came to think that the principle of contradiction does not hold, that we can permit directly opposite positions equal rights, so to speak. Christians in particular have been slow to pick up on the moment when they are themselves under siege and from what quarter. We want to think that contending "values" or, in their corporate expression, ideologies, arise from nowhere. However, they invariably have an origin in the heart of man, in his own relation to himself and to God. If we do not accept God's order, we will form our own. We live in a society that has formed its own order. This is the intelligibility of our social situation. By denying first principles of being, of any source of order outside our own free making of principles themselves, we claim a liberty that is in fact divine, or better, what appears to be divine, since the divine Being is not itself a chaos.

All sin, no matter how small, is a re-enacting of the account of the Fall, of the sin of Adam and Eve. *Genesis* is a jewel of insight into one's own soul. That is, all sin is an attempt to put into existence our own definition of good and evil. When this same effort appears on the public stage, its outlines are the same, though much more dangerous in extent. We forget that to affirm that what is wrong is, in fact, "right" is a choice that is open to us. It puts us into the uncomfortable position of having to defend ourselves, not only against ourselves, but against the order of things. When we affirm anything to be true or false, we *ipso facto* leave ourselves open to questioning. Our claim to reason in our acts can itself be tested by reason.

In this sense, our warfare is against principalities and powers. The intelligence guiding our culture and our souls to accept doctrines and practices directly opposite to the natural and supernatural order in every instance reveals a hatred of God, but a hatred manifested in the goods of man, particularly in the most innocent. It is no historical accident that the life of man in its coming to be and in its ceasing to be is the locus of the rejection of the divine among us. Rather on the part of individuals, philosophers, politicians, and all of us, it is a choice between good and evil, with consequences attacking the core of what we are. It involves the truth of human life which we did not make, but only receive. We hold this truth to be self-evident.

The first step in this process was always to seek out the exceptional case, the most poignant or difficult problem. Killing or divorce was wrong in principle, except in this one case. Finding the truth in such difficult cases, St. Thomas says, is not always easy or available to everyone, but in all actions open to us, there is a truth, if we sort it out. The older prudence itself examined the exceptional case to see if indeed, in this instance, it was murder or divorce. But the new case, basing itself on sympathy or compassion and not wanting to see where the principle led, was that one exception could be found where a genuine murder, adultery, or whatever was all right. At this point we passed over from good to evil. We affirmed that at least in one case, evil was good.

In the second step, we were asked to tolerate the sinner, even if we did not approve of the sin. This tolerance was not just for the exceptional case, but for all cases like it or similar to it. This tolerance seemed well enough until there were a sufficient number of tolerated exceptions. At this point, the language of tolerance changed to the language of rights. We were not only to "tolerate" what was admittedly wrong, but we were to acknowledge a right to do what was tolerated. Thus abortion became a right; euthanasia and suicide will soon be, if they are not already, "rights." But if we have a "right" to certain things, guaranteed by the law, the exercise of that right involved the deprivation of right or liberty of others. Even worse, if my "values" are different and imply that the "values" of another are wrong or dangerous or sinful, then I am being at least "judgmental." That is, I am claiming that my "values" have some priority, some claim to truth against someone else's "values." On the other hand, the "right" to abortion, say, necessarily involves the killing of an incipient human life. This incipient life either has no "rights" or its rights yield to mine. Thus rights are not equal, so that he who controls the definition of rights controls whose rights are and are not observed and enforced. We are back to power.

It turns out that if my list of things wrong includes your list of rights, then I am a threat not only to you, but to the polity that establishes that no preference can be given to one or other value. The polity has to square the circle; that is, it has to deny the principle of contradiction, the principle of being in order to continue to believe in its own theory. In this context, my "values," which are only my options, without any grounding other than my will, and hence can make no claim on another, are "intolerant" by their very definition. The one sin of intolerance involves the claim to regulate my ideas or thoughts that hold that certain activities or positions are wrong and dangerous. Ultimately, we really cannot allow the public criticism of ideas, once considered against the natural law, that now appear as civil rights. The search for the maximum freedom and the minimum coercion ends up with a need to control certain ideas. If all citizens have a "right" to their definition of happiness or value, then they have a right to their good name.

The claim that certain actions are wrong is implicitly a threat to the state, which is designed to prevent strife and which is neutral to all values except to that of intolerance, which begins in the mind. In this sense, the theory is already in place that makes Christians enemies of the state. We simply await its enforcement, either by converting or coercing Christians to live according to secular norms or by marginalizing or eliminating those who insist in calling wrong what the state guarantees as "right."

III.

St. Augustine was a kind of genius about the workings of the sinful heart. He understood that we would not easily admit that what we wanted to do, if it was wrong, was in fact wrong. Indeed, we would seek to justify it as right. The reflections of Augustine on pride are the most profound explanation we have about the workings of our hearts in our efforts to avoid acknowledging that our true good is given to us in our being and in the response of God to our sins. In this sense, all small sins are big sins and all public sins are rooted in small sins. The notion that private sins can be separated from public disorders is hopelessly naive. All social or political sins are rooted in private sins. And what happens to a republic or democracy composed of a multiplicity of disordered citizens, defined in the classical moral sense? They attempt to construct a public order to reflect their own private souls. And this can happen without changing a single name of public order – constitution, law, right, court, congress, senate, president.

Our regime is more and more a regime that institutionalizes and fosters disorders of soul that were classically defined as sins or moral faults. Moreover, it is a regime that does not want to hear that its public or private order can be questioned. Thus, is cannot stand aside peacefully and tolerate those who recall that virtue and vice, right and wrong, are not simply what is defined by the law as permissible. The identification of classical Christianity with "fanaticism" is the next step in eliminating the freedom of Christians and all followers of a Socrates to be what they are.

Augustine stands for the fact that there never will be a polity in this world that is not disordered. The temptation of Christians in the modern world, as Nietzsche intimated, is to be too much like it. A loss of faith has, in a sense, resulted in our not recognizing what the faith was about, namely, that the Kingdom of God is not located in this world. This same faith prevented the ideologies from succeeding. Ideologies were, in fact, substitutes for faith. They claimed to be able to produce this perfect kingdom in this world. Christians should not be surprised that their loss of faith leads to an ungrounded re-emphasis on establishing a perfect kingdom in this world, along with a hostility to any theory, such as Christianity, that rejects this claim as either desirable or possible. But Christians are surprised when they see this logic working itself out in practice.

Chapter V

A MEDITATION ON EVIL

"Turning away from God would not be a defect except in a nature meant to be with God. Even an evil will then is proof of the goodness of nature. Just as God is the supremely good creator of good natures, so he is the most just ruler of evil wills, so that even though evil wills make an evil use of good natures, God makes a good use of evil wills."
– St. Augustine, The City of God, *XI, 17*

"The devil has a huge problem with sacrificial love. He knew God, but he did not love, so he would not serve. With the Genesis *narrative, there is a choice between the Tree of Life and the Tree of Knowledge of Good and Evil. The principle of the Tree of Life, as I see it, is sacrificial love; the principle of the Tree of Knowledge of Good and Evil is power. The essence of evil is a choice of the heart for power rather than the Cross. My husband once told me of some priest who told him of a theory – only a theory of course – that the devil rebelled when he was shown a vision of the crucifixion. He said, in effect, I will not serve a God who belittles himself in such a manner. There are those who do not serve because they are*

so mixed up and poorly formed that they cannot find God. But those who take a deliberate stance against Him usually do so because they hate the Cross. This probably equals what you call wanting to find their own way to God. They want a way which is not self-sacrificial but self-promoting."
— *Tracey Rowland, Cambridge, England, 21 October 1997*

I.

In the Second Book of *The Republic*, we find a brief but impressive remark about the relation of God and evil. Socrates is concerned about the poets, especially Homer, who picture the gods indulging in activities distinctly improper and indeed quite wrong. Socrates does not deny either the incidence of evil in the world or its attraction, but he does not want even to hint, as Homer does, that God causes or participates in evil. Socrates discusses this matter with Adeimantus. But by showing that God does not indulge in evil things, Socrates seems to limit the power of God, who, like Machiavelli's Prince, should be able to do either good or evil, as suits His needs. Socrates, however, asks, "Then good does not cause all things; it is responsible for the things that are good; but not responsible for evil?" Adeimantus agrees to this distinction. Socrates adds, "Nor can God, since He is good, cause all things as most people say. He is responsible for a few things that happen to men, but for many he is not, for the good things we enjoy are much fewer than the evil. The former (good things) we must attribute to none else but God, but for the evil we must find some other causes, not God" (379b–c). Such a passage surely provokes us to wonder about good and evil in their origins. On the one hand, the implied thesis, as indicated, seems to limit the power of God by denying Him causality over evil, while, on the other, it indicates that the cause of evil is not God or the good. Yet, it does not seem valid to maintain that God is "limited" if He does no evil.

Rather He is freed to be good, with no taint of evil. But if the cause of evil is not directly God, it must be found to be properly located in what is not God, yet in what is capable of itself bearing responsibility. If evil were merely a necessity, it would seem, we should not be so infuriated by its very existence among us, if indeed it can properly be said to "exist." The search for a proper "cause" of evil other than God, in any case, stands near the top of all philosophic inquiry about *what is*.

Strictly speaking, however, that about which we can "meditate" is restricted to a something, to some good, to some reality, to something *that is*. What is not a "thing" or not grounded in being, we can only come to grips with in terms of a relation to actual things or in terms of a conscious negation of things *that are*. As such, "nothing" is simply not thinkable. What is not, is not. This negative affirmation is the best we can do for it. But it does affirm what is true. It is true that what is not, is not. Negating the reality of something is a conscious act that takes place in our mind, in its considering the meaning of things. Things that need not be – among which things we must ultimately include ourselves – cause us to wonder. What would it mean, we ask ourselves, if such things that need not exist were, in fact, *not* in existence, were *not* outside of nothingness, as they are outside of nothingness when they *do* exist?

Thus if we endeavor to meditate on "nothing" or on *no* thing, we have first to imagine or experience some real thing. We begin thinking only when we notice and affirm that *something is*. Then, in our own further reflections, we can deprive *what is* of its existence; we can negate its existence. We know in this case of our own negation that reality is not the way we are imagining it when, in our minds, we deny existence to something *that is*. Even to think about what does not exist, we have to form a contrary-to-fact image of what is not. This image substitutes for the normal reality or form of that about which we think when we consider anything *that is*. We are quite aware of what we are doing and of the problematic status of what we ponder. Our thought denies something in the reality about which we think, all the while we know that what is denied in our minds does in fact exist.

Any meditation on evil is an aspect of the meditation on nothingness. It is a meditation on what specifically ought not to exist as it concerns what does exist. Evil is always related to existence, not simply to nothingness. Nothingness, as such, is not evil. If there were only nothingness, there would be no evil since evil always depends on something that exists. Most human beings, even early on in life, will have recognized that something is evil or disordered in the world or, even more strikingly, in themselves. They will have blamed someone for it, excused themselves of it, or been angered about something that ought not to be. The very act of blame or anger or excuse implies some initial recognition of a lack of correspondence between what ought to be and *what is*. Without this awareness of a comparison between an ought and an is, we could not properly blame or praise anything. But we feel justified in our anger at something that ought not to be, but is. Our anger is, or should be, grounded in reality and its disorder.

In the beginning, however, most people, even while knowing they are influenced by it, will have no very sophisticated idea of what evil is. Yet in practice, unless they are intractable determinists who maintain that whatever is must be and must be as it is, they will acknowledge that some things or aspects of reality ought not to exist, or ought not to exist in a peculiar way, even when they do exist, and are known to exist, in the way they do. The reality of evil is not to be minimized or denied as a mere illusion or misperception. Some things could have been and ought to have been otherwise even though they are now what they are. The "presence" of evil falls among the things that could have been and should have been otherwise.

II.

Common sense experience remains the place where we have to begin when we consider more formally or thoroughly evil itself along with other central issues that impinge on our lives. Accounting for reality and for our place within it is a basic requirement of what it is to be a complete human being. We are to "examine" our lives, as Socrates told the Athenians in *The Apology*. Much of mankind's history and several of its philosophers can be our guides, without overlooking the not-to-be-denied possibility of our choosing bad guides. Simply put, no matter who we are, certain things are found in reality that we should have deliberately and systematically thought about. In particular, we should consciously think about the troubling aspects of reality that we identify as evil or wrong. Far from being dangerous to think properly or accurately about evil, it is more of a danger not to seek to understand what it might be or what might be said about it. An education that neglects a meaningful effort to account for evil is a most incomplete education, as no life can fail to confront its perplexing effect on us.

No education is adequate that neglects a fundamental aspect of reality from its ken. Not to have been puzzled by evil indicates a very inattentive and shallow mind. It is no accident, then, that St. Thomas, at the very beginning of the *Summa Theologiae*, a book itself designed for beginners, intimates that evil is one of the major reasons given for belief justifying the non-existence of God. Notice that with this consideration, Aquinas denies neither God, things, nor the problem. The implication is that if we do not understand evil properly, we will never understand God properly. Evil, at first sight, then, by being a phenomenon so obvious that no one would ever bother to deny it, seems to imply that God, as all good, cannot exist if evil exists. No real God, no good God, it is urged, would allow a world in which evil exists. "Is this position true?" we ask ourselves.

What St. Thomas affirms, however, is that what God has in mind may be so great that it involves "allowing" the possibility of evil. To "allow" is not the same as to "cause." The fact of evil, in other words, may indicate, not the *inability* of God to prevent it, but His *ability* to overcome it in His own way in order that something greater might come to be pass. In this sense, thinking about evil is also an aspect of thinking of God. God Himself, it is implied, is bound by a certain order or logic in His own being. Evil, in this context, causes us to wonder what this "greater" good that "allows" evil might possibly be. We already notice, for starters, that the problem of evil forces us to think more clearly about what we think we already know. The very rationality of our being includes the account of evil as "possible" but not good or justified as evil. Paradoxically, as in the case of all revelational positions, thinking about evil enables us to think better period.

No doubt, we begin any discussion of evil with the empirical and unavoidable realization that at least something is radically wrong in our lot, otherwise the problem would not occur to us. But it does occur to us. In fact, it leaps out at us. At the same time, we realize that not everything is disordered, that things in themselves are not evil. We are not Manicheans who think that matter, for example, is to be identified with evil. We do not seek to purify ourselves by escaping from material things as if somehow they were, as such, the cause or definition of evil. Augustine tells us that this Manichean notion that matter is evil is oftentimes a most useful theory if we are trying to justify our own evil acts. It is useful because it puts the blame on something other than ourselves, other than our wills, where it more properly belongs. But Augustine also saw that this explanation of blaming matter would never really work. It was only an excuse for not locating the true source of evil within us, in our wills, not in our being or in our bodies or in the structure of the world.

We understand, at least sometimes, that we can and do use good things in a wrong and evil way. Good things, finite things, are capable of being used wrongly not of themselves but by those who have the power to use them for anything at all – who have "dominion" over them. Indeed, it may well be a duty to use them. In the Book of *Genesis*, we see it affirmed, from the revelational tradition, that no material thing, including ourselves, as such, is evil. Everything *that is*, is good. Or to recall *Genesis*, God looked on all things as He created them and saw that they were not, in spite of being composed of matter, evil, as the Manicheans taught, but precisely "good." The teaching of *Genesis* remains the single most important text for any full understanding of evil. And it begins by affirming that things are not evil in what they are, in their existence. This affirmation includes the human being, limited or finite as he is, and all his given faculties. Evil does not lie in the being of man or in the being of creation itself. Rather, the possibility of evil lies in the fact of created will, of genuinely free will, which itself, as a faculty, is as such good, even when it chooses evil.

If things are not evil, just what "is" evil anyhow? Something mysterious and ominous seems ever to envelop it. The whole messy enterprise surrounding evil, we would like to think, ought not to exist. We long for a purer philosophy, if not for a purer world. We look for a way out. Yet we are loathe to think that nothing at all should exist if the price of eliminating evil means that nothing finite, nothing *capable* of doing evil, could exist. The price of finite, rational existence includes, though it does not necessitate, the possibility of evil. The classic tradition from Plato and St. Augustine affirms that evil is not a thing, but a *lack* of something, a privation. What ought to be there, for some reason of chance or deliberation, is missing.

We are accustomed to hear it said that the devil is evil or that Hitler was evil. But as such, neither the devil nor Hitler is evil in what each is. Unless each remains good in his substantial being, in what he is, he can neither exist nor have any evil attached to him. Evil always exists in, is a parasite of, something good. Ultimately, this dependent status is why evil, or better why its effects, can be overcome. Evil always remains what it is. We can never call what is evil good, because what is evil is never, as such, good. The great lie in the soul is the affirmation that evil is good.

The enduring good that bears evil, however, affords this possibility that good can come about through the good that supports evil's reality. Out of this remaining good, a return path to good is at least possible, though never automatic. It too must be chosen, affirmed. Evil itself remains. It never itself becomes "good." Evil remains eternally what it is, evil, though the being who put what ought not to be into existence can change, can recognize the evil and its definition. And Socrates pointed out that to suffer evil is not to do evil. If someone chooses to do evil, someone else will suffer it. The suffering caused to good beings by someone else's evil is itself potentially redemptive or restorative both to the one suffering the evil and to the one who causes it in the first place, but only on the condition that evil is recognized and affirmed as what it is, evil.

Yet, clearly, some massive truth stands behind the affirmation that the devil is evil or that Hitler was evil. It is as if, which is the case, our being is first given to us for a purpose that is not simply the continued existence of what we are, no matter what it is that we do. What we are presupposes and grounds what we do or how we act because of or in pursuit of what we are. Our existence is itself directed to some purpose that we do not concoct for ourselves unless we claim, as we can, a complete autonomy over ourselves, an autonomy we cannot, in fact, prove ourselves to possess. Our being is ordained to acting, to doing, to knowing. Perhaps it is better to say that we are to direct ourselves to what we are, to the completion of what we are, to choose what we will be on the basis of what we are. We have to will our being in this sense by willing what is good and not by rejecting it or by misusing it. "It is never right to do wrong," as Socrates said. We associate evil with the choiceful rejection of what we are, of what we are invited to be, a choice that is possible in each of our free actions. Every free act bears the potentiality of bringing us to the lack of being that is evil, just as it can bring us to the fullness of being that is good.

III.

The classical writers remind us of the difference between what is called "moral" and "ontological" evil. Not unduly to confuse ourselves by such technical words, both sorts of evil are similar in that they both imply the lack of something that ought to be present. Thus, if I see a three-legged dog, I conclude that some evil has happened to the dog. That is, he is lacking something that he should have but does not. If I do not already know what a dog is, I will never notice that anything is missing if it only has three legs. Until I see other dogs, I will likely think that three-leggedness is proper to dog nature. Let us say that a tree fell on the dog's leg during a storm and cut the leg off. The storm was not evil; the tree was not evil; the falling was not evil; the dog was not evil. The lightning struck the tree and broke the branch. The branch fell and broke the leg of the dog that happened to be running along under it in the storm. Everything here is operating as it should according to its own nature.

The evil in this case of the three-legged dog was fortuitous; it was caused accidentally. Two or three identifiable causes, each doing what it was made to do, crossed at a given time and place. The accident is not directly willed by any of the natural causes, but it still happened because each cause remained what it was. The loss of the leg is evil in the sense that something that ought to be there in the dog is missing. The dog now limps about and cannot run as before. Again, the dog was running down the street for his supper; the lightning struck the tree, the branch fell, the dog lost the leg. Everything was acting according to what it is.

Yet, something identifiable did happen. The dog lost his leg because the tree's branch fell. The dog is missing what ought to be there, and the tree is missing its branch. But that dogs are hungry, that lightning exists and strikes branches of trees, that unsupported branches fall, that they fall on what is there below, these things are good. Everything here is doing what it is supposed to do. We do not want the natural laws that govern these actions as such to be other than they are, for on them the universe of interrelated actions exists.

Moral evil also indicates the lack of something that ought to be there. Moral and physical evil stand within the same general definition of what is lacking in something good. Moral evil implies knowledge, will, culpability, choice. What is lacking in moral evil is the order of good that ought to be there, that ought to have been, could have been put in our actions. If, in a business transaction, I act unjustly, the relation between the other person and myself lacks what ought to be there. The other person is affected by my not placing in my act what should be there. The other person receives an act that is deprived of something that ought to be there – he is deprived of his "due." He in his turn may respond to my evil either by killing me, or by suing me, by suffering the loss bitterly, by forgiving me, or by changing the law to prevent me in the future.

My relationship to the other changes because of my act depriving him of justice. He recognizes this lack of what is due to him. He, rightly in this case, blames me for it. The what-ought-not-to-be-there, the lack, continues in the world until its consequences are stopped, or at least altered or mitigated, by forgiveness or punishment or by the restoring of what ought to have been there. In another sense, however, consequences can never be wholly stopped. The fact that the disorder occurred remains. It is possible, however, that some good can come, not from the evil in the action as such, for it is non-being, but from the even-truncated good in which all evil must exist, including moral evil.

How is it possible that we do evil things? Remember, if we are to be blamed for doing evil things, we must somehow show how this evil act proceeds out of our human powers, out of our reason and will, in such a manner that we are its cause. The moral evil we do refers to those acts we deliberately put into the world in which something due is lacking. Something ought to be there but is not there because we choose not to put it there. What process do we go through in such cases? How do we cause evil to happen in us and through our choices?

Explicitly or, mostly, implicitly, we erect an argument whereby we justify, at least to ourselves but potentially to the world, our acts; that is, we give reasons for them. This "giving reasons" is why, when anyone is accused of doing something wrong, what he invariably does, unless he acknowledges the evil as wrong, is to give a reason, plausible or not, for why he acted as he did. This reason is itself contained in our initial situation of knowing about several ways to do things or several alternatives to guide our actions or at least the possibility of acting or of not acting at all. Socrates said that, given the alternative of death or doing evil, death was better because we did not know whether death was evil, but we did know that choosing to do evil was evil. We establish what we mean by good by indicating what we will die for. To be willing to die for nothing, thus to stand for nothing, also is a course that defines our being. That we have such alternatives in our knowledge always before us whereby we can choose good or evil, is not, as such, evil.

The reason-giving person implicitly uses his power of reason to claim that his reason is the right or governing one not only of his actions in this particular case before him but of all actions in similar cases. The reason he gives for his action is intended to explain his integrity before the bar of reason. By giving his reason, he stands before the bar of mankind's reason. This claim of "reason" is why we can debate or dispute any avowal that would justify an act because we all have the same norm or standard of reason against which to test what is claimed to be reasonable. And the given reason is valid as far as it goes. No one can act without some claim of good or reason in his actions. Evil explanations, in this sense, are parasite to the good in which they exist.

Moral evil does not come about because we acted according to the practical syllogism or argument whereby we sought to put something reasonable in its own order into our actions. Rather moral evil comes about because, in giving our reason to the world and to ourselves for our acting as we did, we fail to mention that we suppressed or avoided examining or illuminating our action on the broader scale in which it really exists. We ate something because it was good, tasty. It was good. But we did not want too much to inquire sufficiently about whether what we ate belonged to someone else. We caused a "lack," as it were, in and by our actions which, to be complete, needed also to consider the justice as well as the pleasure of what is acquired by our act. This lack now becomes, as it were, a missing "part" of our act and incipiently of our character, which is formed by repeated acts.

Our act forever goes forth into existence missing what it should have had. Good is crippled, lacking, by our deliberate choice, something that should be there. It butts up against reality, as it were, with this lack, this what-ought-to-be-there but is not. This lack, as it were, continues to "exist" down the ages and makes a difference in the world *that is*. Once upon a time, there was a dog with a missing leg who was seen limping along by a little girl. Her name was Sarah. Her father was the king. Because she was so touched by the little crippled dog in the storm, she decided to give her life to help the suffering. Her name is now St. Sarah. . . . Evil somehow occasioned good.

IV.

The French philosopher Jacques Maritain brought up the famous query from Origen about whether the devil could, by God's mercy or power, be saved. This effort to "save" the devil is perhaps the most sophisticated form of the denial that evil has any real and ultimate consequences. If the devil can be "saved," who cannot be? After all, it seems unfair of God to be so tough on poor Satan. Besides, does it not impinge on God's power and even more on His kindness if He did not do all He could to rescue from damnation even the worst cases? God did do, of course, all He could do, before the event. If He does anything after the event, however, after the final refusal to acknowledge that evil was evil, it would seem God was not serious in His initial prohibitions against doing evil.

What is implied in this consideration, moreover, is that since the devil is by definition the worst case, it would be much easier for God to save us persistent human sinners who have nowhere near the brains and subtlety of a Lucifer. We like to think that it is liberal or benevolent or compassionate to lessen any finality to any punishment for our acts. We like to think this mitigation or reversal can be done without lessening human or divine dignity as each is originally conceived. The punishment of evil, it is implied, ought rather, *post factum*, to arouse pity in God who is asked to renege on His justice or on His affirmations about the seriousness of our every-day and lifetime choices. In the punishing of Lucifer or of ourselves, we want to accuse God of not being "compassionate," that modern virtue that forgives all, even the devil, by eliminating any criterion for judging actions that are said to have lasting ramifications.

Maritain's solution was one that sought to keep the essential outlines of the basic Christian position on the eternity of Hell and its dire punishment. That is, he does not deny Hell's existence or possibility. He does not even deny its eternity. What he wanted to suggest was a way for God, as it were, to get off the hook by using His own omnipotence. Maritain did not want to deny the devil's pride, but he did want to save him from its ultimate consequences.

Maritain acknowledged that it would be impossible for God to give Lucifer, because of his abiding pride, the Beatific Vision, for which he, like every rational creature, was in fact created. So Maritain proposed something less heinous than Hell but still something apparently compatible with God's goodness and justice. What God could do would be to put Satan in limbo, that place explained in an earlier theology as the location where unborn, un-baptized babies end with that kind of happiness due to finite natures not destined to participate in the elevated inner life of the Trinity. This place was the natural home that would be due to human and angelic nature had it not been granted, from the beginning, the inner life of God as its final and first purpose. This graced purpose, however, seemed to need for its accomplishment, the active power of free choice, in lieu of baptism. Since this choice was lacking in the case of Lucifer, limbo was proposed as a reasonable solution to what appeared to be an insoluble dilemma, the apparent conflict between God's justice and His mercy.

Thus, Maritain thought by analogy, that the devil might be relieved of anything that could be properly called punishment (how angels suffer is itself a question). He would be restored to that natural state of good angels were they not offered the Beatific Vision, which in itself was not due either to their nature or to human nature. Maritain conceived this position out of a spirit that was uncomfortable with the notion of eternal punishment and its supposed dampening of the good name of God's mercy. Maritain, of course, only offered this unusual position as a sort of musing or speculative postulate in his *Approches sans entraves*.[1] He would not have been surprised if he were wrong, but still he felt it would be nice perhaps if God could loosen up a bit with regard to the devil's final condition of eternal punishment and deprivation of the Beatific Vision.

We know from *Genesis* that the devil is a liar. He told Eve not to believe God, all that stuff about death and the eating of the forbidden fruit. Eve, no doubt, had no idea what death might really be like. She was given to understand by the devil that this prohibition of eating of the fruit of the tree of the knowledge of good and evil was proposed by God out of envy, that He wanted to keep Paradise to Himself. This explanation was, of course, another lie. "But why would the devil even want to lie?" we wonder. What he knew for certain in his own mind was that he himself was not God.

We notice that the devil in *Genesis* is following the classic pattern of giving reasons for what he does. These reasons, rational as they appear at first, however, are given in such a way that they do not present the whole picture of the act. When Adam and Eve do accept the deal they are offered, the consequences follow as God, not as the devil, explained to them. But they do not become, as such, as beings, evil. God will use their given being, its goodness, as a basis to repair the damage of their evil in another way. But God's way will not "coerce" them. It will be after the manner of the kind of beings they are created to be. He teaches the free creature to accept and acknowledge the

1 Jacques Maritain, *"ées eschatologiques," Approches sans entraves* in *Oeuvres Complètes Maritain* (Paris: Editions St. Paul, 1991), Vol. 13, pp. 441–78.

evil of his act. He leads him to acknowledge his error and to see what was really the good initially offered for him to do, a good that was subsequently lacking because of the free creature's choice.

V.

The devil, as just remarked, knows that he is not God. His pride may conceivably make him envious or jealous of God, but his intelligence will not permit him to deny the fact that he did not create himself. There was an old novel by Owen Francis Dudley, entitled, I think, *Will Men Be Like Gods?*, a title that serves to illustrate what is at stake here. What is it to be "like gods"? Clearly, pride, the root sin, means that we make ourselves to be the cause of the distinction of good and evil. This was the root temptation in *Genesis*. It is a temptation not so much to be God, but to be "like" God, that is, to choose our way to our destiny, not that of God. Not even the divinity, however, can make what is good to be evil. God is not an arbitrary power, as some late medieval theologians like William of Occam seemed to imply. This god as arbitrary power, already hinted at in *The Republic*, became the "Leviathan" of Hobbes when refashioned for modern political purposes wherein the state becomes the exclusive source of the definition of good and evil, a distinction based on its own arbitrary power.

Maritain's rather amusing effort to show compassion on Lucifer by speculating about God's power does not, in the end, appear to maintain the real dignity of the free creature, angel or man, as well as the simple leaving of the devil where he is destined to go as a result of his own choice and his own definition of what is good and evil. Even if we might imagine that somehow Lucifer has landed in limbo, much to his surprise, wherein he undergoes no angelic "suffering," the fact will remain that he has rejected the gift he has been offered. His being will permanently "lack" what ought to be there. This alone will suffice to define eternal suffering, both of not knowing what it was that God had in mind for those who were obedient and of being locked in oneself as the only definition of reality when one knows that he did not cause himself.

The positive side, as it were, of Lucifer's choice, however, remains. If God intended that other finite creatures, besides Himself, participate in His inner life, it could only be on His, not on the creature's, terms. But, presumably, it would not have been worth God's effort or energies had He not allowed His inner life to be open according to the only terms in which it could be possessed. Since God is love, the only way for Him to become the end or happiness of some being that is not God is for this being freely to choose God in each of his free acts. The form of the virtues, in this sense, remains charity. The free creature's love of God has to be just that, free, and even more, actually chosen as good, as worthy, as infinitely attractive because of what God is.

A philosophic meditation on evil, in other words, is likewise a meditation on good because evil cannot be understood without first understanding that good can be missing from our inner order because of our own choices. The meditation on evil is at the same time a meditation on the ultimate importance of our lives and of our daily actions. When Socrates said that it is never right to do wrong, he implied that it is always right to do what is right when it is presented to us. The presence of what is good causes us not merely to wonder how it happens to be there without our having to put it there, but also to make us wonder about our own incompleteness in our completeness. We are in our very being restless beings, not because we never encounter what is good, but because we encounter it so incompletely. When we seek this completion solely by our own power and definition, we claim a divine power in the little things of our ordinary lives.

"Do you want me to feel secure when I am daily asking pardon for my sins, and requesting help in time of trial?" St. Augustine asked in one of his sermons (#256).

> Because of my past sins I pray: *Forgive us our trespasses, as we forgive those who trespass against us.* How can all be well with people who are crying out with me: *Deliver us from evil?* And yet, brothers, while we are still in the midst of this evil, let us sing alleluia to the good God who delivers us from evil.

We are not secure. We are tried. Things are not always well.

It was Augustine who told us in *The Confessions* not to attach ourselves to "all those beautiful things" in the wrong way, in an evil way. Yet, it is, in the end, he who tells us to "sing alleluia" because we can be delivered from evil. The meditation on evil is not itself morbid or somber, though evil itself is. Socrates said in *The Republic* that virtue can know vice but vice cannot know good. The penalty for vice is the vice itself, the not seeing the good in its fullness, the good that ought to be there. The evil that we do stays in the world. Out of it, out of the good that it lives upon, comes, if we choose it, a yet greater good. In his brief answer to the question of whether the existence of evil made the existence of God impossible, Aquinas was right to cite Augustine: "God, since He is the greatest good, in no way would permit evil to be in any of his works unless He were so omnipotent and so good, that He would be able to bring forth good even from evil." We do not find our own way to God, but God finds His way to enable us, even when we fail the good, even when we do evil, to choose the good and in choosing it, to recognize that it is not of our making, hence we can love it. It is on this basis that we can next consider the truth with our acceptance or rejection of it.

Chapter VI

ON THE WILL TO KNOW THE TRUTH

Why Men of Learning Often Do Not Believe

"We attain to heaven by using this world well, though it is to pass away; we perfect our nature, not by undoing it, but by adding to it what is more than nature, and directing it towards aims higher than its own."

— *John Henry Newman*, The Idea of a University, *I, Discourse V, 1853*

"But we must not follow those who advise us, being men, to think of human things, and being mortal, to think of mortal things, but must, so far as we can, make ourselves immortal, and strain every nerve to live in accordance with the best in us; for even if it be small in bulk, much more does it in power and worth surpass everything."

— *Aristotle*, Nicomachean Ethics, *X, 7*

I.

Several years ago, in 1990, to be exact, some friends gave me for Christmas the Ignatius Press Edition of Newman's *Parochial and Plain Sermons*. This is a book of almost inexhaustible depth and richness. On taking up this book again, I notice that I had, some time ago, put a mark on the Twenty-Fourth Sermon of the First Series. It is called "On the Religion of the Day." It begins, "In every age of Christianity, since it was first preached, there has been what may be called *the religion of the world*, which so far imitates the one true religion, as to deceive the unstable and unwary."[1] Naturally, wishing neither to be "unstable" nor "unwary," I want to be sure that I have some idea of the subtleties of this religion of the world, which subtleties evidently can deceive even the elect because they "imitate" the "true religion." We like to think that the worst evils will look horrid so that we shall easily recognize them, but it is not so. Most often they will be quite enticing and we should not doubt it.

Newman already implies here that no age of Christianity will ever be quite free of this confusion between the true religion and its erstwhile imitators. True religion and truth, no doubt, have difficult going whenever and wherever men dwell. Here, it is intimated that to be successful, the religion of the world must imitate some or other aspect of true religion or else it will never attract anyone. On the other hand, since the imitation is not the true religion, it will contain something that is dangerous, something that will deflect us from the truth while looking rather much like it. We are again surprised that knowing the truth is so difficult. We wonder why.

We suspect at first that truth may be very complex and subtle so that the main problem is simply lack of intelligence or talent, something for specialists, not for us ordinary folks. But we notice, if we are at all sharp, that the cultured and academic unbelievers are many and articulate. It is not the experience of Christianity since its beginnings that the more intelligent one is the more likely one is to be a believer. Yet, Christianity professes to be and is,

---

1 John Henry Newman, *Parochial and Plain Sermons* (San Francisco: Ignatius Press, [1891] 1989), 196.

more than any other, an intellectual religion. "In the beginning was the Word and the Word was with God . . ." Such words from the Prologue to St. John suggest that the world is suffused with intelligence, with word.

II.

Our age has a difficult time with the idea that we are rational beings made to know the truth. We are afraid of truth because it confronts us with our limits, with things that are true whether we like it or not. We like to think we are, in our intrinsic nature, rather raw desires made to "will" into existence what we want, whatever it is we want. Truth, however, implies that freedom is related to something other than itself. Our eyes grow narrowly cautious when we hear, especially from revelation, that it is the truth that will make us free. We think and are taught that it is the truth that will make us "unfree," that truth is a threat to democracy, to what we are, or at least to what we want to make ourselves to be. We have established a culture of choice, not of reason. We do not want to bind ourselves even to truth. At the heart of reality, we hold that things could always be otherwise, not by virtue of their having been created by a divine will, but by virtue of their having no necessary connection with what we choose or limitation of what we want. Things, including our own nature, do not restrict us; we use them as we will. We teach these things in our universities; we live them in our daily lives. We will not admit that anything wrong is the result of what is known or of what is true. Wrong can only mean wrong for me. The "I" acknowledges no other criterion.

Thus, we are perplexed to learn that our happiness consists, according to, say, Aristotle, in knowing and in knowing the highest things. The moral virtues, even in being themselves, are intrinsically ordered to our knowing. We are to know things for their own sakes, simply because it is worthwhile knowing them. In fact, we long to know even if we get nothing further out of it. If there is something we do not know, we seek to learn about it, find out about it. We want to know the world about us. We want, as Socrates said, to know even ourselves, as if there is something about us to know. We want to know about God and who and what He is, once we realize that we did not create or order either ourselves or the universe to be as they are.

Even when we do not use such terms as truth or will, this seeking to know *whatever is* is what we do. We give reasons for everything we do, including, often adamantly, the things that we do wrongly. We cannot not but be rational even when we are acting wrongly. We insist on justifying ourselves, that is, in giving reasons for our deeds and acts, even when we know they are wrong. We are a proud lot. Yet, we worry about what pride is, especially after we have read Augustine, who warned us about it, who told us it was the origin of all vice. We do suspect that we seek to locate the cause of all things in ourselves, not in God. This was Augustine's definition of pride, in fact. Even though we do not believe in the devil, so we say, we know his vice was pride. We are curious about this. What is it that made him a devil instead of Lucifer, the bearer of light, of intelligence? Why is the most dangerous of fallen spirits also among the most intelligent?

III.

The Thirteenth Sermon in the Eighth Series of this famous Newman collection is entitled, "Truth Hidden When Not Sought After." It begins with a famous quotation from *2 Timothy* in which St. Paul disturbingly tells us of those who "turn their ears from the truth," of whose claims to truth shall in fact become mere "fables." Here Newman brings up something that must often cause many to wonder and be concerned about. We know there are intellectual saints. Neither Augustine nor Aquinas, nor Newman himself, nor John Paul II, have need of yielding anything on the line of intelligence to any philosopher or wit of any era. Yet, we also know that Augustine, justly or unjustly, is often said to be the father of most heresies. At one time or another in his life, he embraced about every conceivable intellectual disorder. Thomas Aquinas was not much recognized in his lifetime. Today he is little studied except in a few isolated places. The most intellectual of all popes has unending opposition from what are said to be intellectuals, of indeed intellectuals who call themselves Christians.

Newman, still commenting on St. Paul, points out that if there is religious truth, this implies that there will also be "religious error." He adds that this truth is one so that "all views but one are wrong." Forgetting this centrality of truth, many, even Christians, turn away from truth to embrace "many fables." What are these "many fables"? Clearly, they are alternative explanations of reality, of God, of our redemption and its suffering, of ways to explain us or save us that would not include the revelation that we have received. Newman adds, speaking of his own time, that "all this [embracing of fables or ideologies] is fulfilled before our eyes." Needless to say, the situation is not better some century and a half after Newman. "The multitude of men," Newman observes, "whether by their own fault or not, are wrong even in the greatest matters of religion."[2] This is not an observation of despair about truth, but simply a statement of fact about the reality of the human condition. And it would not be a significant statement unless, in fact, error in religious affairs were indifferent to human living and had no impact on human reality. Newman is willing to "tolerate" religious error, but not at the cost of denying that it is error or at the cost of denying that it makes any difference to our lives what we hold and whether what we hold is true.

If we understand the truth of this statement of Newman, intended, as I said, to be no more than a statement of objective fact, we will be alerted. "This is a most

2 Ibid., 1660.

solemn thought, and a perplexing one," as Newman put it. "How could this be," we wonder, "that most people do not know religious truth?" But there is something that is even more perplexing; although, as Newman said in the light of St. Paul, it ought not to be. It is not just that ordinary people are confused and unknowing about religious truth, but that "men of learning and ability are so often wrong in religious matters also." Here Newman already brings up something that later came to be called the "treason of the intellectuals," not just in religious matters but in matters of polity and morality.

Aristotle had already pointed out that a slight error in the beginning of some science or philosophical position would, if not corrected, lead to a great error in the end. That is, this error would continue in the intellectual community. Its disorder would be expanded, developed, organized; its implications would be carried out in reality. Great systems of errors are often based on a very narrow fault or error, one that seems, to recall Aristotle, small in the beginning. From truth, truth follows, but from error anything can follow, as an old saying went. And of course, even truth can be rejected, though always in the name of another claimed truth.

What concerned Newman is not so much the errors themselves, but the fact that they are made most often by academics, intellectuals, and, yes, clerics insofar as they too belong to the intellectual classes. This deviation of intellectuals concerned Newman because, like Aquinas, he was a great defender of truth and its dignity, philosophic or natural truth as well as the truth of revelation. Newman was not concerned, however, to set up some kind of organization or system to prevent this error from being spoken or propagated. Rather he was troubled by the souls of academics, intellectuals, and clerics themselves, in their deviation.

St. Paul had already warned us that such aberration among philosophers was possible, even likely. Newman knew that St. Augustine himself embraced practically every error imaginable at one time or another in order to justify his life. Newman also knew that Aquinas calmly identified, defined, and explained all the known errors of his time or any time, almost always better than those who promoted them. Christianity is concerned with changing hearts and minds away from error to truth, but after the manner in which hearts and minds ought to be changed, by better thought, by discipline, oftentimes by prayer and a conversion of heart.

IV.

When natural intellectual guides embrace religious error, Newman tells us, "they become stumbling-blocks to the many." That is, they cause and give scandal. They confuse the simple and ordinary folks. Newman is frank, with a kind of refreshing bluntness we almost never hear today. "Let us honestly confess what is certain," he tells us,

> that not the ignorant, or weak-minded, or dull, or enthusiastic, or extravagant only turn their ears away from the Truth, and are turned into fables, but also men of powerful minds, keen perception, extended views, ample and various knowledge. Let us, I say, confess it; yet let us not believe in the Truth less on account of it. I say that in the number of adversaries of the Truth, there are many men of highly endowed and cultivated minds. Why should we deny this? It is unfair to do so, and not only unfair, but also unnecessary. What is called ability and talent does not make a man a Christian; nay, often, as may be shown without difficulty, it is the occasion of his rejecting Christianity, or this or that part of it.[3]

One has only to spend a small amount of time on university campuses, including those that go by the name Catholic or Christian, to realize the abiding validity of Newman's observation.

3 Ibid., 1661.

Newman's point is not, however, that there is something intrinsically at variance between Christianity and intelligence. Quite the opposite, he thinks that their mutual compatibility is itself proof of their own authentic and related insights. The observed opposition, then, must arise from sources other than revelation or intelligence themselves. When Newman points out that "ability and talent do not make a man a Christian," he puts his finger on the problem. Christianity was sent to more than the philosophers, the number of whom will no doubt be very few in any era. The average parish, or university for that matter, is not populated by philosopher-kings. Christ was sent to save not philosophers but sinners, among whom no doubt there might be counted not a few philosophers.

Actually, Newman had in mind not merely the proud professors in Oxford or Cambridge, but also for the local village philosopher who could well display the same attitude of mind that we find in the learned skeptics. St. Paul, in *1 Corinthians*, is worried about the "wise" of this world, and Christ spoke things hidden from the wise and prudent, but revealed to little ones. In other words, no Christian should be at all surprised to find the leading intellectuals of his time confusing him about the truth of revelation or of reason for that matter. We should not be surprised that "men of acute and powerful understandings" reject the Gospel because they think, rightly, that revelation is addressed "to our hearts, to our love of truth and goodness, our fear of sinning, and our desire to gain God's and favor." This is not the stuff of which the intellectual, as such, is made.

The intellectual is interested in something else – "quickness, sagacity, depth of thought, strength of mind, power of comprehension, perception of the beautiful, power of language." Such things are likewise good as far as they go. We may, however, have such intellectual gifts but lack grace or inner goodness. "Ability of mind is a *gift*, and faith is a *grace.*"[4] Here we begin to see how Newman sees the problem. "We just look with amazement on the error of those who think that they can master the high mysteries of spiritual truth, and find their way to God, by what is commonly called reason, i.e., by the random and blind efforts of mere mental acuteness, and mere experience of the world." The reason that can cause such difficulty is a reason that closes itself off from what is beyond reason, yet which likewise contains its own reason, is addressed to reason. The sign of intellectual pride is always that of an unwillingness to consider or to accept what is not merely worldly experience and mental acuteness. What are we to do about this experience of academic blindness to truth?

Newman does not despair, even though he holds no optimistic expectations of it ever being otherwise or of easily convincing proud men about truths they did not concoct for themselves. He is mainly concerned with explaining to believers what they will experience from intellectuals and in warning them not to be particularly bothered about it. Newman's own remedy is quite surprising – respect the intellect for what it is, that faculty of truth that we are given from nature. The fact of its abuse is no cause for us to worry about what it is in itself.

> This should be kept in mind when Christians are alarmed, as they sometimes are, on hearing instances of infidelity or heresy among those who read, reflect, and inquire; whereas, however we may mourn over such instances, we have no reason to be surprised at them. It is quite enough for Christians to be able to show, as they well can, that belief in revealed religion is not inconsistent with the highest gifts and accomplishments of mind, that men even of the strongest and highest intellect have been Christians.[5]

Newman's point is clearly that intellect as such is often a temptation to pride and that many an academic or

4 Ibid., 1662.
5 Ibid., 1663.

intellectual is consumed by it. But intelligence as such is a worthy thing. The fact that some, like St. Augustine or Aquinas, are Christian and intelligent would suggest that the essential concern that we have, whether we be an ordinary person or an intellectual, is how we live, how we respond to the graces we receive. It is not our IQs that will save us, even though we are made to know, to know the truth, and to delight in it.

V.

But it is true that what makes a difference is the way we live. Aristotle already said that our ability to see the truth often depends on our virtue. If we are disordered in our ends, in our choices, we will spend our lives not pursuing truth but rather in shrewdly using our minds to justify what we want to do. Yet, Newman warns us that faith is not easy, even though it is a grace and a gift. We can thus be somewhat disdainful of the academic skeptics while at the same time neglecting the real effort and work it takes for us to know what we ought to know. One of the great problems, particularly in Catholicism, is the very fact of its intellectual richness, a richness that is only rarely and minimally ever seen in an education that includes even doctoral and post-doctoral studies.

The society is filled, in all sorts of disciplines, with the baptized who display Ph.D.s after their names. Yet their religious and philosophical background is almost at the level of a seven year old, if that. Often the highly-degreed reveal the simplest and crudest misunderstandings of basic truths of theology or history. If one's secular knowledge is in radical disproportion to the level of one's religious knowledge, there is bound to be trouble. (This is a problem I have dealt with in my *Another Sort of Learning*.) What Newman says on this point is quite blunt.

> Let us consider for an instant how eagerly men in general pursue objects of this world; now with what

portion of this eagerness do they exert themselves to know the truth of God's word? Undeniably, then, as is the doctrine that God does not reveal Himself to those who do not seek Him, it is certain that its truth is not really felt by us, or we should seek Him more earnestly than we do. Nothing is more common than to think that we shall gain religious knowledge as a thing of course, without express trouble on our part.[6]

No one expects to learn anything else without effort and discipline, so it is Newman's point that religious knowledge is not something that arrives from nowhere, without any effort on our part.

"To gain religious truth is a long and systematic work. And others think that education will do everything for them."[7] But Newman here is not just concerned with the effort that it might take to know religious truth. He also tells us that this truth draws us, attracts us. We have to be prepared to feel its influence on our souls. We do not seek truth just because it is a necessary intellectual exercise. We seek it because we already feel the attraction to the source of truth. Newman can be witty in describing our common foibles and excuses about religious truth that we claim is difficult, uninteresting, or of little meaning to us.

Doubtless if men sought the truth with one-tenth part of the zeal with which they seek to acquire wealth or secular knowledge, their differences would diminish year by year. Doubtless if they gave a half or a quarter of the time to prayer for Divine guidance which they give to amusement or recreation, or which they give to dispute and contention, they would ever be approximating to each other (and eliminate their religious disputes).[8]

What Newman says here is that religious knowledge requires as much attention as any other knowledge. In

6 Ibid., 1663.
7 Ibid., 1664.
8 Ibid.

addition, it requires means that are intellectual and more than intellectual. We know that amusement, recreation, dispute, and contention take up time often better spent on knowing religious truth.

Lest we think that Newman is speaking of a time utterly unlike ours, let us listen to his description of the mind of a man who gives his justification for not honestly thinking through the validity of religious truth. Such truth is difficult to come by because it makes demands on us. We suspect that it will demand of us things we are not presently prepared to undertake. It is difficult because we have conjured up ready-made intellectual excuses that protect us in our implicit refusal to consider truth.

> The present confused and perplexed state of things, which is really a proof of God's anger at our negligence, these men say is really a proof that religious truth cannot be obtained; that there is no such thing as religious truth; that there is no right or wrong in religion; that, provided we *think* ourselves right, one set of opinions is as good as another; that we shall come right in the end if we do but mean well, or rather if we do not mean ill.[9] These positions, of course, while written a century and a half ago, constitute an almost perfect contemporary intellectual description of what most of our contemporaries hold.

Newman's remedy for this condition is, we are astonished to learn, obedience, the most annoying of the commands that the Lord gives to the intellectual of any age.[10] Newman warns us, however, about judging others, even the proud. "Unless we have faithfully obeyed our conscience and improved our talents, we are no fit judges of them at all" (p. 1666). We also know that the variety of philosophies and religions are offered with confidence by

9 Ibid., 1665.
10 See James V. Schall, "On the Most Mysterious of the Virtues: The Political and Philosophical Meaning of Obedience in St. Thomas, Rousseau, and Yves Simon," *Gregorianum*, 79 (#4, 1998), 743–58.

those intellectuals who hold them. How are we to avoid producing our own fables instead of obeying the true religion? Newman's advice is rather in the form of a command or admonition:

> Seek truth in the way of *obedience*; try to act up to your conscience, and let your opinions be the result, not of mere chance reasoning or fancy, but of an improved heart. This way, I say, carries with it an evidence to ourselves of its being the right way, if any way be right; and that there is a right and a wrong way conscience tells us. God surely will listen to none but those who strive to obey Him. Those who thus proceed, watching, praying, taking all means given them of gaining the truth, studying the Scriptures, and doing their duty; in short, those who seek religious truth by principle and habit, as the main business of their lives, humbly, not arrogantly, peaceably not contentiously, shall not "be turned into fables."[11]

If truth must first be sought after, as Newman tells us is the case, our seeking of it must recognize that truth first calls us. We do not create it. We find it, after having looked for it, because we know that we do not possess it by ourselves.

This advice to obey, honestly follow conscience, and pray, we know, is not spoken to us by someone who does not know what intelligence and its temptations might be. Newman reminds us that there are those who are believers and who are also intellectuals. We need not be surprised that many intellectuals do not believe or believe in false gods. This is neither new or unexpected. Yet, it is a betrayal of that good that intelligence can provide for others who do wonder about things and seek illumination about truth from those who claim to know.

But more is available to us about truth than we often are willing to admit if we have not formulated properly the questions for which our minds seek answers. We are all

11 Ibid., 1667.

already redeemed, even those who reject redemption. The way is open; what is lacking is not grace, which is sufficient. Understanding our actual condition is the first step in our quest to know why truth is hidden when not sought after. "We are not under the law of nature, but under grace; we are not bid to do a thing above our strength, because, though, our hearts are naturally weak, we are not left to ourselves. According to the command, so is the gift. God's grace is sufficient for us" (p. 1668.)

The primary sin of the intellectual is not the rejection of reason. The rejection of reason is normally, as in the case of Lucifer, the consequence of the rejection of grace, for once this is rejected then we must create fables to explain why reason and revelation, grace and nature, do not in fact fit together. They do not fit together because we make them so, but because they are so, apart from our making, but not apart from our seeking and not apart from the grace that is sufficient. We are not asked to do a thing above our strength, and our hearts are weak. We are not left to ourselves. The will to know the truth includes the gift that is sufficient for us. The rejection of reason is the drama of our time. It is first a rejection of grace and the patient work that it takes to know religious truth, but above all the will to know it and the humility to accept it.

Aristotle advised us not to follow those who would restrict us to purely human and mortal affairs, however worthy of pursuit they are, as Aristotle himself taught us. We attain heaven, Newman tells us, "by using the world well." Yet, we know that it too "passes away." We perfect our nature not by rejecting it, or making it over into our own image, but by adding to it especially under the guidance of revelation, that teaches us much about ourselves, much that completes the questions we have about ourselves. Men of learning often do not believe because they do not will to know the truth that makes us free. The academic problem is, more than anything else, a spiritual problem – the struggle of pride, grace, and reason. *Homo non proprie humanus sed superhumanus est.* This famous scholastic phrase that we are created for a divine purpose is what Aristotle implied and what Newman taught. The men of learning who do not believe will not to know this truth, the one essential truth that reminds us all that we do not make but are given what we are.

Chapter VII

REVELATION AND "THE TRUTH OF THINGS"

"But the man who is willing to taste every kind of learning with gusto, and who approaches learning with delight, and is insatiable, we shall justly assert to be a philosopher, won't we?"
— *Socrates,* The Republic, #475c.[1]

"Truth is predicated of every being inasmuch as it has being. And this truth is seen as actually residing in all things, so much so that 'truth' may interchangeably stand for 'being.'"
— *Josef Pieper,* The Truth of All Things[2]

"As a hind longs for running streams, so do I long for thee, O God. . . . Send forth they light and thy truth to be my guide and lead me to thy holy hill, to thy tabernacle."
— *Psalm 42:1; 43:3*

---

1 *The Republic*, edited and translated by Allan Bloom, (New York: Basic Books, 1968), 155. "But the one who readily and willingly tries all kinds of learning, who turns gladly to learning and is insatiable for it, is rightly called a philosopher, isn't he?" (Grube/Reeves translation).

2 Josef Pieper, *The Truth of All Things (Living the Truth)* (San Francisco: Ignatius Press, 1989), 35

I.

Catholicism is an intellectual religion. It accepts the principle of contradiction, with reflective insight into the meaning of its denial, as the basic intellectual tool to examine reality, including divine reality. Except for methodological purposes to show that this principle cannot be rejected, Catholicism does not doubt the existence of things or the validity of reason. A religion or philosophy founded in doubt has little attraction for those who know that things exist, for those who do not try to prove the obvious. Reason and revelation, Catholicism maintains, cannot and do not contradict each other. The human mind is made to know truth and does in fact know at least some truth. As such, the mind is at least potentially capable of knowing all truth, *capax universi.*

The human mind is not, however, to be confused with the divine mind. Analogously both are minds, both can address each other. One is not the other. Revelation and its content are directed precisely to mind. Catholicism is not "only" a religion of intelligence, of course, just as man is not "only" mind. Still Catholicism specifically denies that it is itself an ideology, that is, a system dependent solely on human intelligence and will for its content or purpose. Catholicism maintains that it can show in some intelligible fashion that what is "beyond" human intellect is not "anti-intellect." Rather, it is, as it were, *super-intellect.* As St. Thomas put it in his *Disputed Question* on the "Virtues in General," *homo non proprie humanus, sed super-humanus est* – man is not properly human but super-human.[3]

From the beginning, our very existence is directed to more than could be expected of it by its own powers. No purely "human" condition, that is, one un-elevated by grace, ever existed, however much it might have been possible. The "restless hearts" of Augustine and of all those

---

3 Thomas Aquinas, *Disputed Questions on Virtue*, trans. by Ralph McInerny (South Bend, Ind.: St. Augustine's Press, 2000).

who likewise experience this abiding unsettlement at the core of their being are constant manifestations of the natural inability to satisfy our longings. Nothing we encounter in nature will do so, even though all things, including ourselves, are good by this same nature. But that we are called to more than what we are is not an evil or a defect or a denigration of our being but a glory. "Grace does not destroy nature, but builds upon it," to recall a famous phrase from Thomas Aquinas. Even though it be a risk, it is all right to be what we are, and indeed, by grace, to be more than we are. At the completion of what we are, we find not "nature" and things proportioned to ourselves but "gift" and "superabundance," not darkness, but light.

Modern thought, as Leo Strauss once pointed out, even when it gave up on the specific content of supernatural destiny found in revelation, did not really "lower its sights" but merely shifted them to an endeavor to produce ultimate happiness in this world by political, economic, or psychological means.[4] Modern man presumed without acknowledging it the forgotten elevation of grace while, at the same time, he would not admit its necessity for the exalted condition in which he had been created and for which he still sought. The heart remained restless, lacking that which might cause it to rest. Revelation in fact remains obscurely "present" in modern philosophy and politics almost by its very absence, through mankind's constant endeavor to find a perfect society or individual life based upon his own efforts.

In our very act of knowing something, anything, we likewise realize that we are finite, that we are not gods. We are not the causes of ourselves, nor of any of the powers we possess, including the power to know and to will. But neither are we nothing. We are a certain kind of being *that is*. We stand outside of nothingness and know that we so

4 Leo Strauss, *Thoughts on Machiavelli* (Glencoe, Ill.: The Free Press, 1958), 167–68, 281, 296–99.

stand. Indeed, such is our lot, we cannot even know ourselves without first knowing something other, something not ourselves. Some given and particular otherness is what first makes us aware of ourselves. This other remains itself even in our knowing it. We know the real being of the other, however, after our own manner of knowing. Our knowledge does not take something away from the reality it knows, but it does add something to our reality. We are more while what we know is marvelously not less.

The mind is the anti-entropic reality in the universe. Things do not only wind down; they increase with the application of mind to them. We still share some of the awe that Socrates felt when he came across Anaxagoras's principle that behind everything there is not water or earth or fire but mind (400a). The act of knowing something not ourselves, furthermore, enables us to reflect back on ourselves, enables us to be luminous to ourselves. This power of self-reflection is characteristic of a spiritual power, indeed, of a spiritual soul, though a soul whose normal characteristic is not to exist apart from the body but as animating it. This insight too has enormous implications only fully realized with the Incarnation and Resurrection – "the Word is made flesh"; "I am the resurrection and the life."

II.

The doctrine of the immortality of the soul is a Greek philosophical idea, not a prime teaching of revelation, though there are traces of it in Scripture. The philosophical doctrine became important for revelation when the latter sought to explain how the same human being who dies, say Socrates or Mary, is the very person who is resurrected; otherwise we have a problem with our identity both in time and in eternity. Without this understanding of the immortality of the soul after death, we would not have what Christians call a "resurrection" of the same Socrates, but the creation in eternity of a Socrates with no relation to the original. If that could happen, there would be no need for an original Socrates, probably no need for a world at all.

The doctrinal point, then, is that we persist in the same being from conception to forever. This teaching that is a scandal to the Jews and foolishness to the Gentiles remains not only more philosophic but also more romantic than any other explication of our ultimate being. As Aristotle remarked of our friends, we do not want them to become someone else, neither gods nor kings (1159a5–10). Ultimately, we do not want Socrates or Mary to be merely a soul, nor a god nor anything other than what they are, Socrates and Mary. Christianity, from the angle of the doctrine on the resurrection of the body, is the ultimate defense of finite human being and the ultimate ground of human dignity.

Christopher Cardinal von Schönborn, in a lecture he gave in Austria, pointed out that St. Thomas Aquinas had the unique distinction of being the first man who was canonized for no other reason than that he thought, and, I might add, thought correctly. When we praise St. Thomas for thinking, we must not forget that Lucifer was also, after his own manner, condemned for thinking. We are often reluctant to admit that thinking itself, as a moral activity, depends on whether what we think to be true is true. All error and, yes, all sin, I think, arises from our suspecting that what is true might demand our living this truth. Therefore, we avert our attention from the truth in order that we may continue to live as we want. We cannot live this way, of course, when our minds do not support truth so we necessarily erect another, an alternative world for ourselves that prevents us from acknowledging the world *that is*. All error, as Aristotle implied, can explain itself, give reasons for itself, but only provided that it be allowed the privilege of not telling the whole truth which it suspects but does not admit.

Thinking, knowing the truth, knowing why the truth is truth, however, is itself a proper activity of the being of man. This is what it means to define man as precisely the "rational animal," the being composed of matter and spirit who thinks. Thinking does not need to be justified on some grounds alien to itself, for example, that it is "useful" for making something or for doing something, even though it properly does these things also. But our intellectual activities do need to be examined on the basis of the truth of what it is we think. Much of the excitement of being a human being, and it is considerable, depends on the wonder of seeking the truth, on the delight in finding it, and, indeed, in the ever-present danger of rejecting it.

III.

Catholicism, however, is sometimes, indeed often, charged with being rooted in some identifiable falsity, whether historical, philosophical, scientific, or theological. But any such accusation of falsity is itself intelligible. The opposing point can be spelled out and itself examined for its own truth or falsity. This "spelling-out" is at least one of the reasons why we have "intellectuals" within Catholicism. Ultimately, as Plato said, to recall his definition of the truth, we are to say of *what is* that it is, and of what is not, that it is not. To do this identifying of truth and falsity requires far more courage than we might at first realize. Most of the disorders in the universe, as I like to say, arise in the minds and hearts of the "dons," intellectual and clerical, when they claim, explicitly or implicitly, to be themselves the causes and architects of the distinction of good and evil apart from any relation to *what is*.

This positive affirmation of the need of what are called "intellectuals" in Catholicism, therefore, does not deny that these same intellectuals, ourselves not necessarily excluded, are probably the ones most tempted to substitute their own "reasons" for what is called the *ratio fidei*, the reason of faith. No Catholic theology can with impunity ever forget that Lucifer was among the brightest of the angels. Nor can we forget that Chesterton lovingly wrote *Heretics* before he wrote *Orthodoxy*, that he came to the latter through the contradictions he found in the former.

All of this understanding the position of the other recalls the method of St. Thomas, indeed of Plato and Aristotle. Namely, we must be able to state how something deviates from the truth if we would know the whole truth of anything. To put it precisely, to know what error is, is itself a high intellectual good – to know of *what is* that it is, and of what is not that it is not. And we must make every effort to know error and falsity and, indeed, vice. Almost invariably, what prevents us from knowing the truth of things, including revelational things, is not our limited intelligence. Rather it is our suspicion that knowing what this truth is will make demands on us according to which we refuse to live or to follow.

Much of this was already spelled out by Aristotle in the First Book of his *Ethics*, where he indicated the alternatives to a proper definition of our happiness. Once we choose in our souls some deviant end, even though it has as it must some goodness, all our activities will be directed toward it. Soon by long habit we will cease to aver to what we have chosen in all that we do. We will refuse to examine how we live because we do not want to live as we ought.

The honest, objective analysis of any such allegation of falsity in Catholicism, from whatever source, then, is itself a part of Catholicism's self-understanding. Josef Cardinal Ratzinger's recent *Dominus Jesus* was primarily the fulfillment of the Church's teaching about what it itself is.[5] On knowing what it is, Catholicism necessarily also knows,

---

5 "*Dominus Jesus* is found in *L'Osservatore Romano*, English (September 6, 2000), special insert. See James V. Schall, "On Being Faithful to Revelation," *Homiletic and Pastoral Review*, CI (March, 2001), 22–32.

articulates, and affirms what it is not. It does not want to be misunderstood about its very being. At the foundations of Catholicism, we find, not an object of our own making, but something handed down, something we could not possibly have concocted as the purpose of our existence.

One of the most subtle of the objections to Catholicism, as Chesterton put it, is that it is "too good to be true." He was right, of course. This mysterious coherence of all things of faith and reason, of desire and reality, of will and intellect, is the most unsettling thing about what is called Catholicism. It is a dangerous thing to examine honestly, and few examine it. It is unnerving not only to think that it is true in what it says about man, world, and God, but even that it might be true, that its reasons are indeed "reasonable."

What really annoys many critics about Catholicism, then, is not that it is theologically or philosophically "false," but that, on examination, it might very well be as true as it claims to be. It might be capable of grounding and elaborating the basis of its position in a convincing manner, though never in a manner that "forces" our freedom. The truth always must be both known and chosen. We retain the power to reject it. Catholicism, again, professes to be true. It claims that there is a conformity between what it holds and *what is*. No doubt, anything making such a claim to truth today, in a climate of pluralism and skepticism, themselves both philosophical problems in their own right, is considered to be "arrogant," or impossibly uninformed.

But a Catholicism that does not maintain its basis in truth, that does not pass on what was handed down to it as true, would not only betray its own founding; it would also cease to be at all interesting, at all provocative. A Catholicism that can comfortably adjust itself to the tenets and ideologies of this world, no matter what else it is, is not Catholicism. Christ said that He came to cause "division," not peace (*Luke*, 12:49–55). But how does this cause of "division" make sense as an argument for the truth of Catholicism? Only if it did make a difference whether or not what Christ thought about who He is and about how we ought to live was true for everyone, including ourselves. Catholicism, in other words, has good reason to think that what matters is not only what we do, but what we understand and what we think about the highest things.

IV.

Consequently, a Catholicism that presents itself to be but one among many religions or philosophies, and not as the true religion with a foundation in a valid philosophy, is already untrue to itself. The Catholic Church, moreover, has absolutely no objection to other religions or systems that claim that they are the truth. It can deal with such positions on objective grounds. Who, after all, would really care about a Catholicism that held one thing in one generation and its opposite in another or about a Catholicism that said of itself that "it might be true, but was not sure"? Catholicism, in its central understanding of itself, is either true or false; it conceives itself as a whole, as a coherent, unified understanding of the truth about God, man, and the world. This position is not intended to deny any proven truth found in any other religion or philosophy. To recall a medieval controversy, there are not "two truths," one of which can contradict the other. What Catholicism is quite sure of is that the proposition that "all intellectual positions are equal" or that "there is no truth" cannot be true. If the latter propositions are the sole grounds which it must acknowledge to receive political standing or cultural acceptance, it must reject them because they make what Catholicism is to be impossible.

Catholicism does insist on the truth, on the accuracy of its claim as given to it. But at bottom, Catholicism holds that its central revelational doctrines, properly understood, are not found elsewhere. By any comparative

standard, what it holds is unique. No other religion or philosophy has really arrived at the same position with regard
to the heart of revelation, namely with regard to God –
Trinity and Incarnation – and with regard to the world –
creation, Fall, and redemption. Catholicism also holds that
these same revealed doctrines, though they are not the
products of purely human intellect, do address themselves
to reason in such a way as to confirm an authentic philosophy and indeed, on examination, to make it more of itself,
more philosophical. The mysteries of revelation are also
designed to make us think more clearly, this in order that
we might know reality more fully. They accomplish this
clarification when we try to think these truths that are
handed down to us.

An old *New Yorker* cartoon (Breslin) shows a middle-
aged couple sitting on a sofa in their mid-town parlor. On
the table in front of them are two cups of coffee. The gentleman, probably just home from the office, is rather port-
ly, sitting in suit and tie, in a kind of an exhausted trance.
He is staring straight ahead, almost as if he ready to leap
up. His frowning wife at the other end of the sofa is in
slacks, one leg crossed over the other. Her arms are affir-
matively folded. She has blond hair rolled high on her
head, heavy eyelashes, large earrings. Looking right at
him with a cold stare, she is obviously lecturing her husband. "What do you consider your biggest fault?" she asks
him; then after a pause, she continues, "and what are you
going to do about it?" We can be sure that the lady already
knows his "biggest fault." And she also suspects that, as in
the past, he probably will do nothing about it. But there is
no escape for the man. The passage from acknowledgment
of one's "greatest fault" to firm amendment is expected to
be immediate, automatic. No time for confession or repentance. The sinner has no leeway – "What is your greatest
fault? And what are you going to do about it?"

When I ask myself, "why is this cartoon funny?", I cannot help but thinking that it gets at something about the

modern world that is very anti-Catholic. I do not mean "anti-Catholic" in the sense of bigotry, though there is plenty of that around, but "anti-Catholic" in the sense that there is little understanding of the perplexing lot of the sinner, an understanding that stands at the heart of classical Catholicism. When asked why He came into the world, Christ's answer was a pithy "to save sinners." Spiritual fathers, no doubt, have long told us to seek out our "main faults," as it were. St. Ignatius, in his *Spiritual Exercises*, set down an exacting procedure on how to go about this reform. The very structure of the sacrament of confession, moreover, has to do with what we are going to do about our faults and sins. But this stern lady's philosophy is basically "Pelagian." We can get rid of our major faults by a simple act of command by the will. The cartoon is also stubbornly mindful of the difficulty of our doing what indeed we ought to do.

It is often said, with some substance, to be sure, that what most impedes the conversion of the world is the bad example of Catholics who do not practice what they claim they hold. No doubt there ought to be a correspondence between what we think or hold and how we live. Yet, we also can point to examples of those who do not become Catholics because other Catholics do practice what they preach, as it were. Only fanatics, they argue, would observe all the commandments and other outlandish practices required of Catholics. We are more comfortable with lax Catholics, those who do not live up to the Gospel standards. Even a survey of Catholics elected to public office would confirm this. A Catholic known to "disagree" with the Church is more likely to receive the honor of public office than one who agrees, though, happily, we find exceptions.

Yes, it is a church of sinners. Christ did not come for the healthy but the sick, not for saints but for sinners. "What is going on here?" we might ask. Christ Himself intimated that we do not go to the doctor if we are healthy. The modern world, no doubt, with its doctrine of frequent check-ups, has changed the point of this ancient wisdom. I have gone to a dentist for semi-annual examinations for fifty years. The other morning, I had a terrific pain in one of my teeth. My dentist was busy, so he sent me to another dentist. The second dentist tapped the painful tooth with a small mallet. I jumped. He said, "yes, there is something there." After he drills for a while, he tells me that I have a big cavity. I think, "so much for semi-annual examinations." What do I conclude from this with regard to Catholicism's understanding of itself? "Only he who preserves to the end will be saved." That is to say, there is no safe place wherein all our teeth will be solid and only virtue will be practiced. Catholicism does not allow us to think that some political or economic or social program will automatically save us. In the drama of our purpose, of our understanding what we are, is ours.

V.

What about the social gospel? What about justice? What about culture? All of these questions, I think in conclusion, are themselves subordinate to the first question about the truth of things, about the truth of Catholicism. The question of truth comes first, even though living the truth follows on knowing what it is. We will have no social gospel, no justice, no adequate culture if the pursuit and acknowledgment of truth, and truth for its own sake, as the Greeks used to have it, is not also an intrinsic element in their understanding. As I like to put it, more or less following Plato, we can, and many do, save our souls in the worst of regimes and lose them in the best. The risk and drama of our existence take place whatever the condition of the world. The reason that God created and redeemed us is not contingent on our politics, on our social situation. In the Epistles and the Gospels, slaves were saved, almost as if to say that those who were not slaves might well not save their souls.

Catholicism, however, is not a religion of withdrawal from the world. It does think that man has something to do in this world that makes a difference both to the world and to his own salvation. What else could the giving a cup of water to the thirsty mean? Indeed, what else could the invention of a pure water system for public consumption mean? Catholicism thinks things can be better or worse not by themselves but how we stand to them. It also thinks with Aristotle that, very often, when we claim we are making things better, we are in fact making them worse. Our "intentions" are not entirely independent of the worth or danger of the actions that flow from what we decide to do. This possibility that what appear to be noble ideas can produce something quite aberrant, again, is why truth matters, why action is not healthy if it is not grounded in contemplation and truth. And is it possible to construct societies, families, souls on the basis of some untruth, or series of untruths? Of course it is. Does there remain some truth even in the errors? That too is valid but not unless we acknowledge both the truth and the error.

So this is the agenda of Catholicism. It is both contemplative and active, both vividly aware of the city of man and of the City of God. It professes to accept any truth wherever it is found. It also holds that its own peculiar truths are designed not just for itself in some isolated enclave but for everyone. Hence it cannot rest with itself. Woe to it if the Gospel is not preached. Catholicism is not true to itself if it presents itself among the nations as simply "another" religion. But it knows about saints and sinners, knows that each of us, even believers, can potentially be either. We live in a world that does not want to be bothered by the truth. We have a religion that insists that only the truth will make us free. We have minds that are restless and malcontent if they do not find the truth that also seeks them.

Without Catholicism, I think, we could not, ultimately, know who and what we are, men destined to eternity, fallen and redeemed. The story is told of an aunt coming to visit her sister's family. The sister had two small children who eagerly watched their aunt as she opened her suitcase. They were waiting for the presents that they knew she would bring. Finally, the aunt fished out two large, handsome bean-bags, one blue and one red. She said to her little niece, "One of these bags is for Tommy, and the other is for you. Which one do you want?" The little girl promptly replied, "I want Tommy's."

This little story contains the truth of things, doesn't it? We are given gifts we do not deserve, even though we anticipate them. Catholicism holds that this world exists from nothing, that it need not exist, but does. Man is the center of the universe and at his center is his will that must choose even to accept the gift of *what he is*. The fact that we want Tommy's gift and not our own reminds us of the Fall, of our ability to reject what we are given and make the world in our image. We fall and yet we rise again. The Fall is not the last word. The truth is the last word. For this we are made and for this we long. The laughter of our selfishness – "I want Tommy's" – hints that evil and pride are not the last word in our creation. Catholicism is an account of how it all fits together, the truth of things. We may not want to listen to it, we may not want to live it, but it is there, constantly directing itself to our minds so that we might understand what we are and why there is a correspondence between the world and ourselves, between the fact that the world exists and that we can do something within it.

Chapter VIII

"WHY SHOULD ANYTHING GO RIGHT?"

On the Curious Relation of Revelation, Reason, and Reality

"Pelagius asserted that even without divine grace, man could lead a good and happy life. Divine grace, therefore, was not necessary for him. But the truth is that man is actually called to salvation; that a good life is the condition of salvation; and that salvation cannot be attained without the help of grace. Ultimately, only God can save man, but He expects man to cooperate. *The fact that man can cooperate with God determines his authentic greatness."*

– John Paul II, Crossing the Threshold of Hope[1]

"I do not blame in the least those who do not believe in Christianity for combating it with all their might; taken seriously, it undermines all other orders but its own, and it turns its back on the modern relativistic skepticism."

– Thomas Langan, The Catholic Tradition.[2]

1 John Paul II, *Crossing the Threshold of Hope* (New York: Knopf, 1994), 194.

"*The great peril is that the human intellect is free to destroy itself. Just as one generation could prevent the very existence of the next generation, by all entering a monastery or jumping into the sea, so one set of thinkers can in some degree prevent further thinking by teaching the next generation that there is no validity in any human thought. It is idle to talk always of the alternative of reason and faith. Reason is itself a matter of faith. It is an act of faith to assert that our thoughts have any relation to reality at all. If you are merely a skeptic, you must sooner or later ask yourself the question, "Why should anything go right, even observation and deduction? . . . There is a thought that stops thought. That is the thought that ought to be stopped. That is the ultimate evil against which all religious authority was aimed.*"*

– *G. K. Chesterton*, Orthodoxy[3]

I.

If we assemble a child's tricycle from a flat box purchased at Toys 'R Us, or if we put together a new computer from instructions in the brochure, we know the tricycle or computer will work if we make each step in the proper order. The reason that things go right is because we have grasped the order of assembly, itself placed there by whoever shipped the box containing the tricycle or computer. If we miss one or two steps, we find out that the thing does not work or does not work correctly. We assume either a) that the instructions were wrong, or b) that we did not follow them. Some things do work; some do not. We seek to explain the latter by the former, the things that do not work by the things that do. A thing works according to what it is. Though we are neither tricycles nor computers,

2 Thomas Langan, *The Catholic Tradition* (Columbia: University of Missouri Press, 1998), 7.

3 G. K. Chesterton, *Orthodoxy* (Garden City, N.Y.: Doubleday Image, [1908] 1959), 33.

we know that things go right for us and things go wrong for us; otherwise we would have no complaints or no praises. If there were no order of right or wrong for us, we could never be able to tell the difference between what is right and what is wrong. We would never be able to be angry if things went wrong, or pleased if they went right.

One morning, I was taking my daily walk on the streets of Georgetown. On returning, I came to the corner of 35th and "O" Streets, two blocks from the entrance to our campus. It is a three-way stop, with "O" Street continuing on as a one-way street to my back. As I came to the corner, out of my one good eye, I saw that a car was coming to the stop sign just ahead of me. When I saw that it would stop, I walked across in front of it, vaguely keeping an eye on it. When I reached the opposite corner, I heard the car pull across the intersection behind me crossing 35th Street, as I walked on up the "O" Street sidewalk to the campus.

What went on here? Clearly, I was absolutely certain that a car was at the intersection and that it was stopped. I trusted my senses to tell me this information. Also, I was quite sure that I existed and stood on the street corner. Without sight and sound, I would not have known what was ahead of me, unless I also happened to touch or smell the stopped car, assuming that I had these other two senses also. I likewise believed that the unknown driver of the car would not suddenly run me down as I passed in front of his car. Sometimes, when I am not sure a driver sees me, as he may be looking another direction, I will lightly wave or tap the car to be sure the driver knows I am there. If I thought the driver were my personal or class enemy, however, to recall something in Plato about our relation to a doctor, someone, say, who wanted to get rid of me, I definitely would not have walked in front of his stopped car. I presumed, in other words, that before me was a driver who would respect the law and its intention to let this pedestrian, which happened to be me, pass in front of the stopped car in safety.

In this account of a normal morning's walk, we have elements of faith or trust, of the certainty of our senses telling what is before us, of proper estimation of where the car is, of what it can do, of what it is. Basically, before I act, I want to know the truth of *what is* there in front of me. I am, in other words, connected with, plunged into the world in which I act without the slightest hesitation, once I am sure I see and understand what is there before me. I may not, of course, see or hear a fast car coming the other direction, or notice a meteorite falling out of the sky toward my head on the same corner. Each, supposed fast car or meteorite, is doing what it is doing, following its own laws and nature. In that latter case, my attention is elsewhere, I am not seeing what I should be seeing, on the assumption that I want to stay alive. But an accident may happen, or perhaps even a murder, a fact whose causes need to be puzzled out. There is a reality before me, even in my every-day deeds, a reality that reveals to me the truth of things in a world in which I live and act.

I thus inhabit this world in a time and a place, which too are real. If I cross the street two minutes after the car leaves, I will not be hit. If I cross the street on 35th street, while a car is crossing the same street on 34th street at the same time, it won't hit me. I trust my senses and my judgment to tell me what is actually there. And they do tell me. Logically, if I am standing on a corner, one morning, but in theory if I doubted the connection between my senses and my mind, I would never move, on the assumption, of course, that I was aware that I myself existed and that I could be hurt by something outside of myself.

But if I never move because of my uncertainty about what was there in front of me, I would have to wonder just how I got to the corner in the first place. Indeed, I would even have to wonder how I knew what a street corner was. In short, in this account, I am pondering, in Chesterton's acute phrase, "why does anything goes right?" Even if I supposed that the world were a dream, I am quite confident that I would still try to jump away from an oncoming car. That is, if I thought the world were a dream, I would still act as if the dream were real, that cars still knock us over in this world even when my theory only claims it is a dream.

II.

For almost a century, it has been the suspicion of acute minds like that of Chesterton that in the end, because of certain basic propositions at work within modern thought, the only thing that would save reason from itself would be revelation. He thought that doubts about the instrument of reason, about its power to reveal to us what was not itself, would become so strong that we would have to make a blind act of faith to affirm that the grass was green or even that it was grass. When Chesterton said in *Orthodoxy* that "reason itself is an act of faith," he did not mean that reason itself requires for its own validity some scriptural proof, granted that some scriptural passages do suggest that our minds do know things.

When Christ said on the Cross, "I thirst," for instance, we have no doubt that He did in fact experience a need that is normally satisfied by drink. The soldiers who gave Him bitter gall to drink certainly understood this. When He said "I thirst," He did not mean "I need a smoke," or "My legs hurt," even though they did. We think His affirmation was about thirst even if we ourselves might doubt whether Christ ever existed or ever suffered on the Cross. On the hypothesis that any human being was so crucified, we would expect him to thirst, even if it never happened. We would affirm that reality has connections with our minds even when we think something does not happen.

What Chesterton meant by saying that reason depended on "faith" was that reason could not go back to an infinite regression of rational "proofs" for its integrity. There would come a beginning, an *arché*, in which it was quite clear that the thing either is or is not. A thing could not be and not be at the same time. All faith ultimately depends on someone who actually sees. Faith may be blind, but it is not stupid. It is grounded in some reality that someone sees. Faith testifies to the validity of the reports of this seeing.

Truth, as Plato said, is to say of *what is* that it is, and of what is not, that it is not. We cannot "prove" the affirmations that *what is* is and what is not, is not, by some other clearer "proof." These things are self-evident. But we can try to deny them. When we do try to deny them, we will find ourselves constantly affirming the principal in our very denial. The minute we maintain that our reason is not rational, we affirm a truth about our reason. We are forced to affirm what we want to deny, in order to deny what we affirm.

This is all very amusing. It is something that everyone can understand with a little effort. But even more basic, it is something, as Aristotle had said, that everyone simply assumes and knows in all that he does and thinks. When Christ said, for instance, "see the lilies of the field, how they grow," He meant that a) they were lilies, not roses, b) that the flowers were growing and not dead, and c) that He knew that the lilies existed and were seen. Furthermore, He knew that they were so beautiful that not even Solomon in all his glory was arrayed as one of these – which suggests He also knew something of the raiment of Solomon as well as of Solomon himself.

III.

In recent years, I have argued that Catholicism has never been intellectually stronger or culturally weaker. This position is, if you will, a paradox, counter-cultural even. In view of recent scandals among the clergy, including the bishops and their use of or lack of use of authority, this cultural weakness seems almost overwhelming, something sinister. What is meant by a cultural weakness? The word "weakness," of course, by itself implies no moral culpability, and I do not want to exclude moral culpability from what I mean by cultural weakness. It may in fact be a primary component.

In some things, weakness is a virtue, a good. We say "strong as an oak" or "like a rock," but also we speak of "a reed shaken in the wind" or a "helpless baby." We know that in some cultures petty thievery is frequent, or abortion, or AIDS, or graft, or lying, or shoddy work. These are almost never without fault; they are not just "weaknesses." They contain the essential element of will. A living culture does not and cannot exclude some criterion, independent of the culture itself, by which its own worth is evaluated. All cultures are, in this sense, "open," even when they choose to be closed.

Culture is not a "thing," of course. The center reality of our existence and our culture is a person who chooses freely to act this way or that. But culture indicates a pattern of thinking and action that result in laws, customs, habits that a people actually lives by. We can live by the truth. But we can also live by falsity which we usually also call truth. We can even enforce what is wrong by laws, opinions, or customs. In either case, whether in truth or in falsity, how we live will appear as an element in our culture. And how we live reflects how we think, what we hold as true. In this sense, every culture already contains within itself ignorance, diffidence toward the ways of truth, and choices of what is evil, necessarily under the rubric of some good. It will also contain virtues, worthy institutions and customs.

What the recent expositions of internal moral disorder within the Church has emphasized is not merely that we are a Church of sinners – itself a dogmatic truth – but a Church in which at least some of its members, including the clergy, maintain that what the Church teaches as true is not true or are not capable of being lived as true. What has confused so many, Catholics and non-Catholics alike, both those who love and those who hate the Church, is the evident lack of any use of authority to address the issues that are broadcast now with regularity within the media and culture. The general impression is that, while the Church may teach what has been handed down, it does not enforce its own teachings so that people wonder how serious the Church is about itself and what it says it teaches.

Chesterton had said long ago that no one is surprised if a monk breaks his vows. One does not need to be a genius to understand this. What is astonishing is rather obedience to vows, something that is claimed to be impossible and indeed unnatural. It is easier to explain why we sin than why we do not. And there is a very cold and realistic view of the world, Augustinian, that would expect that, for the most part, things will go wrong. Such is the consequences of the Fall, even among the faithful. In recent years, no doubt, we have tended to de-emphasize this more realistic aspect of the faith, only now to see it come back in a much more troubling manner. If we look at what has happened to the Sacrament of Penance in most churches, it almost appears that we proclaim ourselves to be a sinless people.

We ask ourselves, "is there anything in Catholic doctrine that would lead us to think that widespread corruption in the clergy *cannot* happen?" If we know anything of the history of the two-thousand-year-old Church, we know that corruption has happened before. The Church survived and will do so again. But the historic scandals left their mark in the form of schism or apostasy or other political or social disorders. Sin is always punished somehow, even when it is forgiven. "What is done in secret will be shouted from the housetops" now seems to be almost a daily occurrence. The forgiveness of sins does not mean that our sinful actions do not continue with their results in the world in some fashion. Nor does it exempt us from civil laws. God can bring good out of the good in which all sinful acts must exist. He does not obliterate the sinful acts put into the world even if He forgives sins.

But while Christianity is a religion that conceives itself to be composed of saints as well as sinners, it is not a religion that is designed to foster sin. To be sure, it is supposed to define sin. It is also supposed to be a religion of the forgiveness of sin. But sins cannot be "forgiven" unless they are acknowledged for what they are. They both deny principles of order and act the basis of such denial. This is why there can be no forgiveness without first acknowledging the validity of the law or rule violated by the sinful act. This structure of norm, choice, act, repentance, punishment, is the foundation of all drama. Every life is also a story in this sense.

IV.

With un-characteristic German wit, Nietzsche, in *Beyond Good and Evil*, has an amusing comment on how "unphilosophical" the English are, especially their most famous philosophers, Bacon, Locke, and Hume. "What is lacking in England and always has been lacking," Nietzsche observed,

> was realized well enough by that semi-actor and rhetorician, the tasteless muddlehead, Carlyle, who tried to conceal behind passionate grimaces what he knew about himself; namely what was *lacking* in Carlyle – real *power* of spirituality, real *depth* of spiritual insight, in short, philosophy. – It is characteristic of such an un-philosophical race that they should cling firmly to Christianity: they need its discipline if they are to become moral and humane (#232).[4]

Nietzsche, no doubt, did not necessarily think it was a good idea "to become moral and humane" after the Christian

---

4 Fredrich Nietzsche, *Beyond Good and Evil*, trans. R. J. Hollingsdale (Harmondsworth: Penguin, 1972), 164.

manner. He seems to have thought it a noble idea, but he was disappointed in how Christians lived. If it was "philosophy" that gave us "real power" and "real depth of spiritual insight," then the English did not have the courage to live with the will to power by which we could overturn our morals. Christianity, in this view, becomes a creed of cowards. To be "moral and humane," which Nietzsche thought would happen to Christians because of their disciplined doctrine of weakness, was still firmly un-philosophical. Yet, Christianity, be it noted, is an intellectual religion; it does not denigrate intellect. It will not be treated as a sentiment or a feeling or a myth.

Nietzsche quipped that "the last Christian died on the Cross." There is some truth in this witticism. Certainly the best Christian did die on the Cross. But taken strictly, the aphorism is a denial of the very purpose for which Christ died. There are many popular theological theories about today that seek literally to save everybody, whatever they hold or whatever they do. The doctrines of forgiveness or mercy or justice, even when they retain their orthodox Christological understanding of how this universal salvation is possible, are stretched so far that no one is in fact condemned. If this is true, our lives become considerably more secure and considerably less dramatic, considerably less interesting. What difference could it possibly make what we did or thought if in fact we were all saved? But if we go back to Nietzsche's aphorism about the last Christian, if it be true that the last Christian died on the Cross, it would also follow that the Incarnation was utterly useless, and if the Incarnation was useless, then so too, it seems, was creation, itself an expression of that Word in the beginning that was made flesh. Today, the Church is locked in a theoretical struggle about whether, ultimately, anything, particularly Catholicism, makes any difference whatsoever.

In *Fides et Ratio*, John Paul II discusses the importance

of a philosophy of being. In typical Thomist fashion, he seeks to understand both the truth and what is the consequence of denying it. He even touches on the centrality of Nietzsche's will to power. "*Nihilism* is a denial of the humanity and of the very identity of the human being," the Pope writes.

> It should never be forgotten that the neglect of being inevitably leads to losing touch with objective truth and therefore with the very ground of human dignity. This in turn makes it possible to erase from the countenance of man and woman the marks of their likeness to God, and thus to lead them little by little either to a destructive will to power or to a solitude without hope. Once the truth is denied to human beings, it is pure illusion to try to set them free. Truth and freedom either go together hand in hand or together they perish in misery (#90).

If there be no objective order in being, including human being, we lose "the very identity of the human being." If the human face reveals its soul, which in turn reveals the image of God in which each person is created, then we deny the dignity of what we are if we deny any order or substitute our own norms for what is given. Freedom is a consequence of truth, not its creator.

V.

An old *New Yorker* cartoon shows a serious TV executive in a huge, elegant office, the walls full of posters of various stars and celebrities. The boss is wearing a pin-striped suit; he leans against his desk, hands in his pockets. A young man is sitting in a comfortable chair before him, relaxed but looking anxiously at the executive, who tells him, "I'm sorry, Mel, but we're letting all our anchormen go. Our viewers don't want any more news."[5]

5 *The New Yorker Cartoon Album: 1975–1985* (New York: Viking, 1985).

One is struck by this last sentence, "Our viewers don't want any more news." It is quite amusing. Yet, what if we changed the scene a bit. Let's suppose the executive is a bishop and the anchorman Mel a zealous cleric. The bishop says, "I'm sorry, Mel, but our congregations don't want any more *good news.*" This transposition brings us to one of the major issues of modernity, namely, the fact that people do not want to hear the *good news.* It is one thing if they cannot hear it because their political authorities will not let them consider it. This is the case in much of the world today, in fact. In a good part of the world, the *good news* cannot be presented because the political system prevents it, because it is against the culture. In other places, while not totally preventing it, the public order severely restricts it. In still other places, any claim to truth, especially religious truth, is looked upon as a sort of fanaticism, a danger to the state if not to the mind. Religion, especially Christianity, is to be so private that it can have no visible expression.

Is it possible for people not to want *good news?* In one sense, we maintain that everyone is searching for that which will ultimately explain himself to himself, make him happy. At the radical core of our being is the awareness that we do not explain ourselves to ourselves as if we caused our own being. The Christian has no problem with the fact that something exists. He does not want to be himself the total explanation of himself. He does not conceive his freedom to consist in defining himself to be what he is, whatever it is. He suspects, like the man assembling the tricycle or computer, that there is an order already contained within his being. Freedom means the impetus to find it. And yet, if we suspect that there is an order in creation that we ought to live by, and we choose not to live by it, as we can, then it is to our interest not to hear the *good news.* Any effort to call our attention to some order we do not choose to follow will be looked upon as an intolerable interference with our freedom.

When I remarked earlier that the intellectual case for Catholicism has never been stronger or its cultural position never weaker, I had in mind the fact that also at work in the culture is a system of denials or better refusals. Culture is never merely neutral. We often hear that Christianity can be adapted into any culture, that it can accept what is good in any culture. While this may be true, we cannot forget that each culture also contains elements that are contrary to human dignity or intelligence. These differences are often officially sanctioned, held with jealous passion, quite dangerous to challenge. It is not enough to be of good will and to find what is right. We must admit what is wrong to be wrong. This is the constant danger that the effort to go forth and teach all nations runs into. The popular tendency is to blame Christianity for not appreciating another culture. But part of the purpose of Christianity is to teach what is true to the benefit of cultures that lack some part of it. I would maintain that behind all of the controversies about poverty, ecology, war, politics, and truth lie issues of the truth of things.

An editorial in *The Wall Street Journal* (July 8, 2002), entitled "Arabs and Democracy," cited the United Nations Human Development Report. The report was refreshing in locating a problem that has something to do with religion and culture. There are no democracies in the Arab countries. "The 280 million citizens of the 22-nation Arab League produced a combined GDP of $531.2 billion in 1999 – less than Spain's. . . . And if the average annual growth rate of just 0.5% over the past two decades continues, it will take Arabs 140 years to double their income, while other regions will achieve that in less than 10 years." The *Journal*'s solution is that the Arab states lack both democracy and freedom. This is no doubt true, but it seems that behind all of this is a theological problem that prevents any meaningful understanding of freedom and democracy. If the essence of Allah is will and hence no secondary order can exist in nature, then the incentives and presupposition for growth are lacking. We may praise the culture for certain things, to be sure. We need not deny our own faults, but there is no avoiding the problem of the complete truth that must be considered in evaluating any culture.

If we are nihilists, of course, we will simply write off the Arabs as fanatics. But if we are Christians, we still see the importance of the long controversy that St. Thomas began in the *Summa Contra Gentiles* about the truth of things, including the truth that lies in revelation. In denying precisely the Trinity and hence the Incarnation, in preferring simplicity to complexity, we think that there are secular consequences to an incomplete understanding of God. In a relativist multi-cultural culture, this is not a popular view, as it assumes that there are truths in Islam and things that ought to be there but are not. It may not be polite to point these things out, but never to confront the issue of truth and its completion is to abandon the human enterprise in its glory and completeness.

VI.

The subtitle of these considerations is the following: "On the Curious Relation of Reason, Revelation, and Reality." What the Catholic mind implies, indeed affirms, is that these three sources belong to each other, even though reality never needed to happen, and revelation is a gift. Reason is likewise a gift of whatever it is that caused man and mind to be in the first place. Even if we are Hegelian determinists, we have to account for these sources of information about *what is*. What is "curious" about these things is that they do not contradict, but reinforce, each other. Reality, *what is*, does not explain itself and when it tries to do so, it must rely on reason. When reason explains reality, as it naturally seeks to do, even delights in doing, it constantly comes up against questions that it cannot itself answer.

But reason presents real questions. Why revelation is curious is that it seems to be directed to the very questions reason proposes but for which it cannot find clear answers. This seeming coherence does not, in itself, "prove" that revelation is true such that any mind can see the relationship. That would be heretical. What it does mean is that we cannot exclude the fact that something in reality seems to address what reality proposes but cannot answer. We cannot but be astonished at this unexpected relationship. It leads us to something beyond ourselves, but something that is addressed to ourselves.

"The metaphysical proofs for the existence of God are so remote from the reasoning of men, and so complicated, that they make little impression," Blaise Pascal wrote,

> and if they should be of service to some, it would be only during the moment that they see such demonstration; but an hour afterwards they fear they have been mistaken. *Quod curiositate cognoverunt, superbia amiserunt.* [What they knew by curiosity, they lost by pride.] This is the result of the knowledge of God obtained without Jesus Christ; it is communion without a mediator with the God whom they have known without a mediator. Whereas those who have known God by a mediator know their own wretchedness. (#542)[6]

What Pascal said contains much truth. It is true that the proofs for the existence of God are difficult for most, even, experts fear, an hour later. Those who can understand them still see them as speculative demonstrations. Pride and curiosity are often mixed with our pursuit of knowledge, especially knowledge of the divinity.

A knowledge of God without Christ is possible, but it is a dry knowledge. No mediator exists for the philosopher. Probably it is not wholly true that people do not know their

---

6 Blaise Pascal, *Pensées*, trans. W. F. Trotter (New York: Modern Library, 1941), 172.

own wretchedness without a mediator. In his *Politics*, Aristotle himself spoke of our "wretchedness" just on the basis of observation and in the *Metaphysics*, he thought nature seemed to be "bound" somehow. But it is true that we know our wretchedness better if we know that Christ died on the Cross for our sins, if we know, in other words, the last Christian was a mediator to explain ourselves to ourselves.

Let me recapitulate the themes that I have wanted to stress here. Each of the five propositions is worth considerable reflection, each reveals something of the argument that I have sought to present here.

1) Ultimately, only God can save man, but He expects man to cooperate.

2) "Taken seriously, (Christianity) undermines all other orders but its own."

3) *"Quod curiositate cognoveunt, superbia amisereunt."*

4) "Our viewers don't want any more news."

5) "Why does anything go right?"

The one thing that seems to be missing from this list, something at the heart of all reality and all revelation, is the wonder of it all. Wonder is the first and most inciting of human experiences, not just the wonder itself, but the suspicion that wonder leads to intelligence and vision about *what is*.

Near the end of the third volume of *The Lord of the Rings* Gandalf makes the following remark, apropos of those who want to know the future ahead of time itself: "Many folk like to know beforehand what is to be set on the table; but those who have laboured to prepare the feast like to keep their secret for wonder makes these words of praise louder."[7] Such words, of course, could well be a description of divine providence about the meaning and unfolding of

---

7 J. R. R. Tolkien, *The Return of the King* (New York: Ace, n.d.), III, 271.

the human lot. We do seek to know what is *to be*. Not everything is yet known or revealed to us. We live in a state of expectancy, even if we live in the state of sin or a state of virtue.

Plato already understood that what the world was most lacking for its completion was not more creation, not more reality, but someone within reality to praise what existed, what is to be. The secret seems to be kept to us so that we might wonder and that we might, in the end, praise *what is*. We are comforted to know that if something can go right, it is possible at least that all things are going right. It is because of our misery, as Pascal said, that we know that we are saved. The last Christian died on the Cross. It is no mere accident that He was also the Word made flesh who dwelt among us. It is not a necessity either. It is a gift like *all that is*. And this brings us to the question of the purpose of this gift.

Chapter IX

ON THE PURPOSE OF
"THIS WORLD"

"God in Christ was reconciling the world to Himself, not holding men's faults against them, and he has entrusted to us the news that they are reconciled."

– St. Paul, 2 Corinthians, 5:19

"All you nations sing out your joy to the Lord."
– Antiphon, Week III, Sunday, Readings,
Roman Breviary

"Honored as I am with a name of the greatest splendor, though I am still in chains I sing the praises of the churches, and pray that they be united with the flesh and the spirit of Jesus Christ, who is our eternal life; a union in faith and love, to which nothing must be preferred; and above all a union with Jesus and the Father, for if in him we endure all the power of the prince of this world, and escape unharmed, we shall make our way to God."

– St. Ignatius of Antioch,[1]
Letter to the Magnesians.

---

1   St. Ignatius of Antioch, Bishop and Martyr, (40–107 AD), Letter to the

I.

The term "this world" can have many meanings – a scientific meaning referring to the physical cosmos, a theological or a moral meaning. In the citation from St. Paul, "the world" was in the process of being reconciled to God through Christ. Such a reconciliation implies some fundamental disorder, something had gone wrong. Paul pictures the world as longing for its redemption as if somehow it also was affected by the Fall, or even by its own finiteness. "The whole world is waiting for God to reveal his sons," Paul wrote to the Romans. "It was not for any fault on the part of creation that it was made unable to attain its purpose, it was made so by God. From the beginning till now the entire creation, as we know, has been groaning in one great act of giving birth." (8:18–22). So the world itself, as related in the creation account in *Genesis*, had to be essentially good, not evil, in order for such a reconciliation to take place.

Nonetheless, the sins and faults of men affected both themselves and the world. They evidently could not be reconciled by human power alone, since they themselves had, in their very being, a transcendent destiny not of their own origin or making. "This world" likewise could be seen as that spirit or mood in the human soul, found constantly in history, that set itself against God. In this sense, as St. Ignatius of Antioch told the Magnesians, the prince of this world had power so that, "to make our way to God," we needed to see that Jesus Christ is "our eternal life" to which nothing, not even the good things of this world, are to be preferred. This was likewise a constant teaching in St. Augustine. The alternatives to the City of God always consider something finitely good in the world to be fully capable of satisfying the human heart, a position that Greek philosophy, Christian revelation, and human experience itself deny.

Magnesians, found in the Roman Breviary as Second Reading, Sixteenth Sunday in Ordinary Time.

We are thus more or less familiar with this terminology by which "this world" can mean several different things. What I want to examine in this chapter is the status of "this world" itself. That is to say, what is the ultimate purpose of what goes on in the world? What ultimately is it that we see when we see before us the right and wrong activities going on in this world? Is it about the rise and fall of nations? Is there merely some inner-worldly purpose? And what would it be?

The antiphon speaks of "nations speaking joyfully to the Lord," but we know that nations as such do not speak or sing, though we might hope for a nation that allows us to fulfill our ultimate purposes as human beings in peace – not all do, as we know. We may have heard of the Hegelian expression that "a happy nation has no history." We do find singing in happy lands.

But if we look over the world, both now and in history, we do not find too many happy countries. Indeed, we are constantly being warned, even by our religion, to be concerned with the dire conditions of poverty that we find in the world as well as by the moral decline in our own culture. John Paul II, at Czestochowa on 4 June 1997, remarked, "we live in times of chaos, of spiritual disorientation and confusion, in which we discern various liberal and secularizing tendencies: God is often openly banished from social life . . . and in people's moral conduct a harmful relativism creeps in. Religious indifference spreads."[2] This is not a happy scene.

Recently, moreover, I was rereading C. S. Lewis's famous book, *The Problem of Pain*. It remains one of the best analyses of this delicate subject of suffering and pain, one that does not exclude the question of the Cross itself. In the first pages of this book, Lewis recalls his own atheist days. When asked, "why are you an atheist?" his response was that the evil in the world is what justified this atheist position. How so? "Their [human] history is

2 *L'Osservatore Romano* (June 18, 1997), 7.

largely a record of crime, war, disease, and terror, with just
sufficient happiness interposed to give them, while it lasts,
an agonised apprehension of losing it, and, when it is lost,
the poignant misery of remembering it," Lewis summa-
rized his position. "Every race that comes into being in any
part of the universe is doomed; for the universe, they tell
us, is running down, and will someday be a uniform infinity of homogeneous matter at a low temperature. All stories will come to nothing."[3] No God, supposedly, could have
caused such a world; therefore, there is no God.

II.

St. Thomas himself likewise tells us that the principal
argument against the existence of God is the presence of
evil in the world (*Sum. Th.* I, 2, 3, ob.1 and ad 1). The argument is that surely an all powerful and all loving God who
intended the good and happiness of rational beings in this
world would not have allowed the presence of evil.
Therefore, if there is a God, this God is "responsible" for
evil. But God could not be imagined to cause evil. Therefore
we do not have to believe in Him because, on such a
hypothesis, He could not exist.

St. Thomas's answer to this line of thought, following St.
Augustine, is straightforward. God does not "cause" evil,
but only "allows" it. God would not have allowed evil, furthermore, had He not been able to bring a greater good
from it. Even evil somehow serves the good. What is this
greater good? Basically, it is that God could not offer "eternal life" to a creature except on the condition of that creature's capacity freely to accept it. God is bound by the conditions of what He wants to do. In other words, the only
being really capable of appreciating the glory of God would
itself have to be not God, a creature not determined in its
response to the good. But this entails, in other words, that
it would be possible for a free creature to reject God's offer
to it to live at a level higher than could be expected of it in

3 C. S. Lewis, *The Problem of Pain* (New York: Macmillan, 1962), 14.

its natural status. This position presupposes that from the beginning, God intended to create the world in order that the free creature might reach the elevated end offered to him.

Without this initial purpose there would have been no cosmos, no world. What this view means is that God did not first create this world, then, as an afterthought, decide to do something with it, namely, put free creatures on it and offer them a status that would include some participation in God's own inner-life. This very offer would require from the beginning a special grace to make this possible. Thus, to recall again a phrase from St. Thomas's question on charity, "*homo non proprie humanus sed superhumanus est*" ("Man is not by nature natural but supernatural"). More than anything else, this statement explains just why it is that we cannot ever properly speak of having an "earthly paradise" as our only and ultimate end unless it also includes angels' or man's free relation to God and what He has planned and offered to the human race.

Now, it is quite possible for some high good to be offered to us but that we still reject it. We necessarily refuse it in favor of some other good – hence, as we have seen earlier, the classical definition of evil must always include the notion of "lack" in some otherwise good being, a lack caused primarily by free will. Such choice of one good over another happens to us all the time, in fact. Moreover, the revelational offer of God to men is not pictured in Scripture as being something neutral or indifferent, something that we are morally free to take or leave. Looked at from this angle, God seems to be quite serious about what He offers to mankind. The offer is not on a take–it-or-leave-it basis as if it made no ultimate difference to us or to God what we choose. Scripture speaks of this destiny as something to be taught to all men. There is even a certain urgency to this mission, even after two thousand years.

Indeed, one of the first orders of business in the Church today is to reaffirm the priority of its obligation to preach the full Gospel to all men whether or not they accept its fullness. The very nature of religious freedom implies that making this teaching known is itself a good, whether it be accepted or rejected. This is particularly important in our multicultural era which, from various angles, rejects the idea that this redemptive purpose and mode are possible, obligatory, or necessary. This is what *Dominus Jesus*, the recent instruction about what the Church teaches about itself, was about.[4]

In his lecture in Rome on the occasion of the tenth anniversary of the publication of the Encyclical, *Redemptoris Missio*, Francis Cardinal George remarked that "in recent years, the Pope's focus on Christ the Redeemer appears to be motivated by a growing concern that the waning commitment to mission *ad gentes* reflects a crisis of faith – faith in the central mysteries of our religion: the Incarnation, the Redemption, and the Holy Trinity."[5] The Church must state clearly from time to time just what it holds and why it holds what it does hold. It can do so in terms intelligible to men of any era or place. Most people simply do not know what the Church holds about itself; nor do they have any coherent idea of the logical and philosophical coherence of what the faith proposes. Catholicism, again, is also a religion of intelligence. Other people, however, do know what the Church holds, but they reject one or another of its tenets. Others still try to make as if everyone already, at least implicitly, holds and practices what it teaches, or, worse, that it does not matter what we hold as it makes no difference for our final destiny. Again, Catholicism is an intellectual Church with clear and defensible reasons for what it holds and why it makes sense to hold it.

4 Declaration of the Congregation for the Doctrine of the Faith on the Unicity and Salvific Universality of Jesus Christ and the Church. August 6, 2000. *The Pope Speaks*, 46 (#1, 2001), 33–52.

5 Francis Cardinal George, "One Lord and One Church for One World: The 10th Anniversary of *Redemptoris Missio*," *L'Osservatore Romano* (January, 2001), 7.

III.

The immediate occasion of these remarks in this chapter arises out of two somewhat disparate experiences. The first is the result of teaching a class of some ninety students each semester for twenty years. In this class, I always read, among other things, Herbert Deane's provocative book, *The Political and Social Ideas of St. Augustine.*[6] In it, we find a frank discussion of what Augustine holds to be the state of mankind as the world comes to its eschatological end as described in Scripture. Augustine does not think that things will get better and better. He is definitely not a "this-worldly utopian." Indeed, he doubts if very many believers will still be found in the world at its ending. Furthermore, Augustine thinks that ultimately few, even among believers, will be saved. Needless to say, no doctrine can cause more outrage among the modern thinkers than this one that suggests that what they are presently doing will not save them, no matter what it is.

Let me cite just one illustrative passage to catch the mood of Deane's presentation of Augustine. Deane writes:

> Augustine . . . does not assume that growth in church membership or influence can be equated with an increase in the number of those men who truly love God. Indeed, as history draws to its close, the number of true Christians in the world will decline rather than increase. His words give no support to the hope that the world will gradually be brought to belief in Christ and that earthly society can be transformed, step by step, into the kingdom of God.[7]

These are blunt words to any modern ear, especially when combined with Augustine's view that, in the end, very few will in fact be saved. On considering these ideas, however, we should not forget that Augustine is also the author of *The City of God*, a book, perhaps more than any other, that

6 Herbert Deane, *The Social and Political Ideas of St. Augustine* (New York: Columbia University Press, 1956).
7 Ibid., 38.

describes the beauty of what we are offered, if we would choose it.

Invariably, when modern students read such words of Augustine or anyone who stands in his tradition, they will be distinctly bothered. They will frown a lot, incredulously. They simply cannot believe, even as a proposition to be considered on the evidence we have, that "few will be saved," or that things are not getting better. Nor can they believe that we cannot make the world better by our own efforts; after all to make things better is why they think they are going to college. Is not this what we have been doing, that is, making the world "safe for democracy," as a famous American president once put it? Not a few wonder if the world is not safe precisely because of democracy.

Reading Augustine, however, is often the first time the typical student has ever been asked to consider the real condition and purpose of "this world." It requires an enormous self-blindness to think that, from God's eyes, the world is in fact getting better and better. There is a lesson to be drawn here from this deep unsettlement with the thought that this world may in fact be as Augustine maintained. The lesson is not that there is no hope, but rather where is it that the source of hope lies? Is it really apart from the inner soul of each human person and the final destiny he is offered from the beginning?

Augustine, I point out, is pretty much an empiricist. He does not, in fact, delight in condemning people to Hell. Nor does he deny that he may be wrong. His view on how many are lost or saved is conditioned by his own observation of how men act in the world at least up until his time, though I suspect that he would doubt if our time is much different in principle. Moreover, Augustine does not think that God is cruel or unloving. Just the opposite. His clear understanding of what love is, more than anything else, leads Augustine to the conclusion that in fact few do love something above themselves. We can take one of four positions about what we see in "this world": either all people are saved no matter what they hold or do, or most are saved, or few are saved, or none are saved. Augustine held for the third position, that few were, in fact, saved. That none are saved is contrary to the faith, while that all are saved, though conceivable, as writers from Origen to von Balthasar have held, is not likely.

If, I point out, Augustine were to read a morning newspaper in any major city in the world today, he would find little evidence that his general assessment of the number saved, based on empirical observation, needs modification. He would see displayed there in the morning press the same lusts, wars, crimes, hatreds, greed, dishonesties, and lies that he saw in Carthage or Milan, or Rome. It is amazing to me how quickly students, when confronted with this example of the morning newspaper, become less hostile to Augustine's thesis, even when they suspect that what he says about human disorder also applies to themselves.

IV.

The modern student trained by the modern mind in these questions does not, on reflection, really think that what Augustine saw in "this world" is inaccurate, just as what St. Paul saw was not an erroneous description of the social facts. Most students are horrified by what they often see on their years abroad or in what they read in class. They want to "do" something about it, usually, alas, go to law school. But they do not think that this "doing" something has much if anything to do with how they think or live. And they usually think the task of refashioning the ills of the world to be a "scientific" one of relatively easy effort after embracing the right political or economic formula. The tolerance principle – that all thoughts and actions are equal – means, however, that they will accept no notion that a "right order of things" exists and demands their response on objective grounds.

Moreover, little thought is given to the "first principle and foundation" that St. Ignatius Loyola stated at the beginning of his *Spiritual Exercises*, namely that our first task is to "praise, reverence, and serve God and, by these means, save our own souls." There is actually a notion that we can save the bodies of others without first attending to our own souls. Put it in another way, most students in our culture, as well as the culture itself, shy away from any idea that there is really a truth corresponding to human nature and to *what is*. Or to put it inversely, some levels of action and culture are definitely anti-human, the principles of which are found operative in the presuppositions and agendas of their own souls in their own culture.

What people want to hear is that even if they do any desired thing, even if they define sins as virtues, as we do today, usually in the name of human rights, there are to be no ultimate consequences of anything we do. What most seem to want is a world of no risk, of no consequences. If we want God to take the risk out of our world so that nothing we do makes any difference, so that we can believe or do whatever we want with no untoward results, then what we have logically done is to remove any reason for our being created as free human beings in the first place. So at this stage, I should like to say that what goes on in this world is the carrying out in history of the risk that God took in creating creatures. He made for themselves. But in making them for themselves, He made them to return to His own inner Trinitarian life which is being offered to each. Any effort to deny Augustine's point about the seriousness of our acts in order that we might not have to worry about their consequences does not enhance but destroys human dignity.

V.

The second experience that I should like to recall has to do with the death of my mother's last sister. My aunt died in Iowa in May, 2001, at 98 years old; she lived the twentieth century. My family on both sides came from a small town in Northwest Iowa. Both sides of the family were numerous so that I have many relatives who have already died. After the Funeral Mass of my Aunt, the funeral cortege drove ten miles across rich corn and bean fields back to the town cemetery. As I looked at this familiar spot, I could see the graves of my great-grandparents, my grandparents on both sides, aunts, uncles, cousins, my own mother. On the tombstones were names of people I had known or had heard spoken of. An Iowa graveyard in the springtime is usually well taken care of, peaceful, a record harkening back down the ages of those who once lived there in all their deeds and beliefs.

As I looked at those graves, I realized that no one here was of any national or international importance, though each was of eternal standing. Most lived their whole lives on farms or in this small town. Maybe some made it to other places, soldiers especially. What strikes me about this little town and those who lived there – as it must of any little or large town that we might know – is that what is important in these lives is really not the record of their work or accomplishments except insofar as these were generally outer signs of a person's inner life. So when I again ask the question, "what is the purpose of 'this world'?" in this context, I think that the real drama is about what sort of life these people lived. Did none, some, most, all save their souls? If they did, it means that the ultimate drama of life, against which little else makes any difference, is taking place anywhere and everywhere. In this regard, I am always struck by Christ's dealings with the little towns in which he grew up or in which he visited – Nazareth, Chorazin, Bethsaida, and Capharnaum. He worked miracles in these towns, more so, He said, than those the people of Tyre and Sidon had seen. He warned them that it would not go well with them. "What could such insignificant people have been doing to warrant such a castigation?" we wonder. (*Matthew* 11:16–24). Neither Rome, nor Athens, received similar warnings, though Jerusalem did.

In an old *Peanuts*, we see a very little Linus, not much more than a year old. He is sitting on the floor quietly sucking on his bottle. In the next scene, he is startled. He looks up to see Lucy walk by. She has a determined look on her face. "Nothing that's going on in the world today is my fault," she announces to everyone, particularly to an amazed Linus. In the third scene, Linus has a glum look on his face after hearing this astonishing information, while Lucy walks by him now with a placid, rather self-righteous countenance. In the final scene, Linus suddenly becomes alive. He has figured out that Lucy's denial that anything is her fault equally applies to him. So he hoists his bottle in the air and happily shouts, "I'll drink to that!"[8]

What goes on in "this world?" Underneath all the secular history and drama of the world, what really is happening, as we see in our cemeteries, is that people are deciding, within their lives, whether they will choose God or reject Him. Lucy's thesis that "nothing that's going on in the world today is my fault," though spoken with great paradox in her case, is a modern Rousseauist version that maintains that no personal or human acts are important. Institutions are at fault. Obviously, the dour Lucy thinks something is wrong in this world. She denies that she has anything to do with it. All human actions, it is said, are conditioned exclusively by structures and laws, not by personal free will. What is important is not what we do or hold but what organization or cause we support.

The division of good and evil passes not through our souls, whether rich or poor, intelligent or dull, but through the institution to which we belong. People are rich or poor, good or bad, because of someone else's fault, not even someone else's personal act since all acts are equally tolerable, but because of some institution or arrangement. Change that arrangement, it is said, and you will change man. The

---

8 Charles Schulz, *Don't Be Sad, Flying Ace* (New York: Topper Books, 1990).

only problem with this well-worn thesis is that human nature remains the same under all institutions. Evil reappears no matter what the configuration of the world. The heart of the world remains in the human soul. But where is this human soul?

Robert Kraynak, in his remarkable book, *Christian Faith and Modern Democracy*, a book that again calls Augustine to our attention, considered the rise of New Age religions and the incapacity of Christians or anyone else to look much beyond success or failure in this world. Kraynak writes that

> such trends are not primarily imposed by the coercive state (though some are aided by it); nor do they triumph by insisting that other more noble activities are forbidden (one is always free to choose). Rather, they triumph because of widespread doubts about the real existence of a transcendent order of Being and Goodness beyond the material world and uncertainty about any higher purpose to life than middle-class careerism and popular entertainment. In most modern democratic societies, these are the only activities that call forth energy and commitment; all others are excluded by skeptical indifference and by demands for immediate sensations that seem harmless because they rarely lead to outright persecution. Instead, the dominant culture is imposed by the social tyranny of public opinion that, in principle, may be rejected but rarely is because the higher alternatives are treated with contempt or are simply forgotten.[9]

This was likewise a theme that Eric Voegelin also touched on when he remarked that the rise of modern ideology into the form of a this-worldly eschatology was largely caused by a failure of belief of Christians in the real transcendence objects or goals of their faith.[10]

9 Robert P. Kraynak, *Christian Faith and Modern Democracy: God and Politics in the Fallen World* (Notre Dame, Ind.: University of Notre Dame Press, 2001), 28.

10 Eric Voegelin, *Science, Politics, and Gnosticism* (Chicago: Regnery, 1968), 85–114.

What all of this means about the purpose of this world and the personal status of each human person before God must be seen in the light of Augustine's belief that, judging from their acts, few were in fact saved. In the light of the myriads of small and large town graves in all parts of the world throughout history, graves that reflect the existence of lives in which the ultimate drama of choice took place once and for all, we must conclude that the ordinary lives of ordinary people are likewise scenes of the greatest risk. This is why the mission *ad gentes* is of such abiding importance.

VI.

Joseph Cardinal Ratzinger, in his *Salt of the Earth*, responded to the question of whether the Enlightenment idea of necessary progress of this world toward "truth, beauty, and goodness" was tenable. He responded, "redemption is always related to freedom. This is what you might call its risk structure. Redemption is thus never imposed from the outside or cemented by firm structures but is held in the fragile vessel of human freedom."[11]

What this means, in conclusion, is that the purpose of the world is the risk of God's initial decision in creation, that is, to associate other free, but necessarily finite beings with Himself, in His inner Trinitarian life. Whether this comes about in each particular life is what goes on at all times and in all places. Nothing can be automatic or apart from individual choice, however related to others it is. The Commandments are precisely to be kept. We can never really say, contrary to Lucy, that "nothing that goes on in this world is my fault." And if there are things that are our fault, this is why we have the particular mode of redemption we are given.

11 Josef Cardinal Ratzinger, *Salt of the Earth: The Church at the End of the Millennium*. An Interview with Peter Seewald (San Francisco: Ignatius, 1997), 218–19.

The great questions of the status of the nations, looked at from the vantage point of the City of God, are not important except insofar as they reveal the choices, the ultimate choices, of individuals in their living and dying in all times and places, even in small cemeteries in out of the way places in Iowa. This is why every small town, every small parish, every apparently unimportant life is significant and remains, as do the supposedly great towns with their great men and women, the locus of what goes on in this world. This is always the choosing of where we stand before God as manifested in our deeds and our understandings about *what is*. Augustine thought few chose well. Modern ideology tells us it does not make much difference how we choose, for our choices, at most, cause "progress" but not personal salvation.

"Man was created to praise, reverence, and serve God and by this means to save his soul" – to repeat Ignatius's famous affirmation. This remains the principle and foundation of what goes on in this world. This is the exact place of the risk that God took in inviting, not demanding, our acceptance of that initial invitation to eternal life. Even God had no choice but first to create us, then to see how we might choose. This invitation can be accepted. It can be rejected. Ultimately, what we choose – and all choices have particular objects – makes all the difference in this world, and in the next. For it is this world in which the ultimate risk of God can take place, the risk that some might not choose to love Him, the more exalted risk that some, many or few, might so choose to love Him. But the ultimate things, as we shall see in the next chapter, are for their own sakes.

Chapter X

"WHAT SAY YOU OF THE PEACOCK'S TAIL?"

Of Things for Their Own Sakes

"For six days you shall work, but on the seventh day you shall rest."

– Exodus *34:21*

"There are branches of learning and education which we must study merely with a view to leisure spent in intellectual activity, and these are to be valued for their own sake; whereas these kinds of knowledge which are useful in business are to be deemed necessary and exist for the sake of other things."

– *Aristotle,* Politics, *1338a10–12*

"He [an old friend] once maintained the paradox, that there is no beauty but in utility. 'Sir,' said I [Johnson], 'what say you to the peacock's tail, which is one of the most beautiful objects in nature, but would have as much utility if its feathers were all of one colour?'"

– Boswell's Life of Johnson, *II, 459*

I.

In the three citations with which I have chosen to begin this chapter, such words are found as "rest," "work," "leisure," "intellectual activity," things "for their own sake," "things necessary," "business," "utility," and "beauty." In the subtitle, I also included the term, "sport," which is derived from Aristotle and Plato and is intellectually related, though with distinctions, to the terms "leisure," "relaxation," "work," and "rest." Two of these words, "work" and "rest," have revelational origins, though they are also found in the classical authors. Some writers, like Hannah Arendt, in *The Human Condition*, even want to distinguish between "work" and "labor," on the grounds that work refers to making things, while labor refers to bodily functions as when we speak of a woman in labor when bearing a child.[1]

Moreover, these terms, with the experiences they represent, bear some intelligible relation to each other. An order exists among them. Saint Thomas says at the beginning of his *Commentary on Aristotle's Metaphysics*, something he repeats at the beginning of his *Commentary on the Aristotle's Nicomachean Ethics*, that *sapientis est ordinare* – it is the nature of the wise man to order things. Indeed, the whole philosophical function is, as Robert Sokolowski has remarked, precisely to distinguish things one from another and so put them into order, to see how they are related in being.[2] All these terms stand in the light of an orderly philosophic understanding of man, his purpose in the world, and his ultimate meaning. Let us see if we cannot spell out together the various senses or meanings of these words, the experience on which they are grounded,

1 Hannah Arendt, *The Human Condition* (Garden City, N.Y.: Doubleday Anchor, 1959).
2 Robert Sokolowski, "The Method of Philosophy: Making Decisions," *The Review of Metaphysics* LI (March, 1998), 515–32.

and on their inter-relationships. This clarification is, I think, intrinsically fascinating – a word that itself has origins in Greek and Latin cultic experience, that which is interesting in itself, for its own sake.

Initially, I will approach my topic through sports or play. Aristotle contrasts the term "sport" or "play" with the term *"theorein"* or "contemplation." He finds that the best way to begin to understand what we mean by the awesome word "contemplation" is to commence with the more familiar experience of sport, which he assumes to be familiar to us. And his emphasis is, surprisingly, not so much in playing the sport as it is watching the game being played before us – not that Aristotle or the Greeks had anything against playing a sport. The Greeks, after all, did invent the Olympic games. The spectator experience is not unrelated to the similar beholding of a tragedy or comedy in a Greek amphitheater. Aristotle calls a game, a sport, something that exists "for its own sake." It is this latter phrase, "for its own sake," that relates it to contemplation, which he considers to be our highest, most delightful, and most profound act. It is also what makes us free through knowing *what is*.

Aristotle notices that sport and contemplation differ in that contemplation, as he puts it, is more "serious" or, perhaps better, beholds a higher object or drama. He recognizes, however, that games are also played "for their own sakes," but they are human constructions or events. Neither games nor human life itself "need" exist, even when either does exist. That is, neither games nor human life cause themselves to be what they are. As anyone knows who understands the rules of, say, bridge or soccer, the regulations are too intricately contrived to be merely accidental. Even a chance game like craps or dice has rules. Yet, as I like to say, watching a good game is the closest that the average man ever comes to pure contemplation. What does this mean? It means that there is a certain hush, a certain absorption in watching a good game, as in watching a play or listening to a concert. During the performance of such games or plays, no one hardly breathes or munches on popcorn, since, as Aristotle said, he is so enthralled in what passes before him.

In such cases, we are taken out of ourselves, as it were. We lose track of our own existence, except our clear awareness of our heightened interest directed outside of ourselves. We literally leave our ordinary time and enter into the time and motion of the game being played before us. We are immersed in the ongoing drama of the game whose result we do not yet know, whose rules and whose setting are fixed arbitrarily, yet finally. We must know and play according to rules we did not make. The winning or losing or both are likewise "according to the rules." We may cheer or laugh or even weep during the game or drama, but we are involved in something for its own sake, something we did not make. We are only indirectly, as it were, concerned with ourselves. We can reflect later that it is we ourselves who were watching this game, this play. We remember that we were there. We have found something that, for a time, takes us outside of ourselves, that involves us in something fascinating in itself. Whether this experience is the final of the World Cup in Madrid, the Super Bowl in 1989, the finals of the NCAA basketball tournament in Atlanta, or just some grammar school county championship in softball, the essential experience is there for us to reflect on.

II.

If we have this experience of beholding a great game even once in our lives, we will be able to take the next step. Play is like unto contemplation, not work or recreation. It is taken for granted that most people, most of the time, spend most of their waking hours in what is called "work." Work has two meanings. First it can refer to what Aristotle calls, in Book 6 of his *Ethics*, "techne," that is, art or craft, the making of things that need not exist, useful things, beautiful things. Their form and shape result from human purpose and human craft. We tend to distinguish the fine and the practical arts or crafts. Fine arts are physical things – words, music, statues – that have no use other than themselves. At their highest, they approach the beautiful, the *pulchrum*, the thing that, when seen or heard, pleases because of what it is, because we see the harmony of its inner form.

Work in its normal sense of "going to work" or "business" or heavy labor is a good thing. It is not the highest thing, but it is a good, human thing. Recreation normally means the relaxation that we need to go back to work. Its end is related to our physical nature, that it cannot continue to work without respite – even games have "time outs." The purpose of work is the making of things we need, that we concoct for our use or pleasure or even for our contemplation. There is nothing wrong with such activities, unless, of course, we think this is all there is to them. This is how Aristotle put the problem: "Amusement is for the sake of relaxation, and relaxation is of necessity sweet, for it is the remedy of the pain caused by toil (work): and intellectual enjoyment is universally acknowledged to contain an element not only of the noble but of the pleasant, for happiness is made up of both. All men agree that music is one of the pleasantest things, whether with or without song . . ." (*Politics*, 1339b15–21). Amusement is for the sake of relaxation which, in turn, is for the sake of work – and remember that in Book 4 of his *Ethics*, Aristotle says that there is a virtue, no less, of being properly amused. But work, though it is a good thing, is for something else. We work, Aristotle tells us, so that we might have leisure. "What is this 'leisure?'" we ask ourselves. Is it not just another word for relaxation? The whole political and moral order exist, in Aristotle's view, in order that we might have leisure, the space for the highest things.

Josef Pieper's famous book, *Leisure, the Basis of Culture*, remains fundamental in understanding what goes on here.[3] Pieper immediately points out that the Greek word for leisure *skole*, the word from which significantly we get the English word "school," is understood to be the opposite word to their word for "business," which is simply the negative of leisure, "a-skolia." The Latin has the same distinction – the word for leisure is *otium*, while the word for business is its negative, *neg-otium*, the same word we have for negotiate. So anyone who is in business, who is "working," is not at leisure. One hesitates to think of what the Greeks would make of our "business schools," to them a veritable contradiction in terms! The activities of leisure and those of business or work are quite different, though they are both human acts and necessary in a complete understanding of man. Our modern priorities seem almost to be the opposite of those of the Greeks, the significance of which goes back in early modernity to Descartes, Bacon, and Machiavelli, to the replacement of the theoretical with the practical intellect as man's highest function.

To grasp these points more clearly, let us take a brief look at Scripture. We will recall that the Commandment tells us to "keep holy the Sabbath Day." Generally, this meant that we were not to work so that we might devote ourselves to something higher, something requiring all our attention. Those of you who are Jewish will recall the strictures that are considered necessary worthily to celebrate this day. Christians are admonished to abstain from "servile" work. Why was this? In part, it had to do with the *Genesis* account of the days of creation. On the seventh day, the Lord "rested." The Sabbath was intended to imitate this example. The positive side of this Commandment implied that there was something more important than

---

3 Josef Pieper, *Leisure: The Basis of Culture*, trans. G. Malsbary (South Bend, Ind.: St. Augustine's Press, 1998).

work or our ordinary affairs, something to which we ought at regular times to turn our attention. And this attention was to something that we ourselves did not make but only discovered, something more fascinating than our own affairs.

Does that mean there was something wrong with "work"? Not as such, of course. Indeed, work was conceived to be something in part "imposed" by the Fall – man is to work "by the sweat of his brow." This suggests that there are two kinds of work – there is that natural activity of man that would have been present even if there had been no Fall. Presumably, men would have still been able to and have wanted to make beautiful and useful things. Moreover, even now, if we are engaged in making something, say a chair or even a house, we become absorbed in it, not unlike in a game. The time passes; we actually enjoy the "work" involved and do not look on it as a burden, just as athletes in fit condition do not notice the exhausting strain on their bodies during a good game.

Another kind of work exists that is drudgery, something boringly repetitive that slaves and businessmen did. They attended to things that had to be done lest human life fall apart. Aristotle in a famous passage suggested that if the statues of Daedalus could move by themselves, they could be constrained to make cloth automatically, for instance, then we would not need slavery or burdensome work. If we know the subsequent history of the industrial revolution, there is something prophetic in this remark of Aristotle. Much modern technology is designed to relieve the "burdensome" side of the work that we need or want so that we can devote ourselves to higher things.

III.

But what I want, mainly, to do here is to see if I can make clear what is meant when we say that something is "for its own sake." Let me recall another passage from Aristotle, this time from his *Rhetoric*: "To be learning something is the greatest of pleasures not only to the philosopher but to the rest of mankind, however small their capacity for it; the reason of the delight in seeing the picture is that one is at the same time learning – gathering the meaning of things." *(Rhetoric*, 1448b13–17). Every human activity, including intellectual activity, has its own pleasure intrinsic to it. What human culture means essentially is to associate an activity with its proper pleasure. But the pleasure follows the act, which act is what determines its own moral status. When we separate the due pleasure from an act in which it belongs, we corrupt both.

Craft activities, even though they begin in us and are carried through our minds to our hands into the thing made, end in precisely the thing made. When we finish making something, the thing remains, while we go away for the rest of our lives. In moral affairs, something rather is found that we "do" as opposed to "make." We judge a person more by what he does than by what he makes or says. Tell me what you get angry about and I will tell you what you are. We are not concerned with merely keeping alive. Plato wrote in the Fourth Book of the *Laws*, "We do not hold the common view that a man's highest good is to survive and simply continue to exist. His highest good is to become as virtuous as possible and to continue to exist in that state as long as life lasts" (707d). If you will, granted that we already are what we are, that is, human beings and not turtles, we have a lifetime project with regard to ourselves, to make ourselves not to be what it is to be men or human beings, as we already are that, but to be good men, as Aristotle says.

What does this mean? It means that I am responsible for what I make myself to be. My moral actions do not have a result only outside of me as craft products do, but also in me. If, say, I rob someone of a vast amount of money, and if I do not repair or repent of my act, I now become within myself someone who has this character of disorder in my soul. I am creating a habit in myself that indicates how I will normally choose to act in similar situations. I am defining what I mean by my own happiness – in this case, presumably, someone who thinks of money as his end.

But the moral and political virtues, while real and worthy in themselves, things that we ought to acquire and not their opposite vices, are not themselves what we are ultimately for. This brings us back to the notion of leisure and rational activity. The moral and political virtues exist also that we may know how to live in leisure. They free us from ourselves so that we might be able clearly and calmly see what is not ourselves. If we get this order wrong, we will never experience what this contemplation is, which is to know the things *that are* for their own sakes.

What do we do when all else, all the necessary things, are done? This is the question that the concept of leisure poses to us. Aristotle says that the purpose of a doctor is to restore us to health, but when we are healthy, the doctor has nothing to say to us. What are the activities of health, the things we do when we have done the necessary things?

In *The Republic* of Plato, there are a number of famous incidents in which the young potential philosophers are listening to Socrates who will be speaking familiarly and calmly to them. Suddenly, Glaucon or Polemarchus or Simmias will stop him and say, "What did you say, Socrates?" They will suddenly hear something that they never heard before. This stopping, this turning around, is precisely what Socrates intended to happen. Each of us, I think, needs this experience in our souls. This is indeed why we are here. Listen to how Plato describes this experience, "This isn't, it seems, a matter of tossing a coin, but of turning a soul from a day that is a kind of night to the true day – the ascent to what is, which we say is true philosophy" (521c). What we do in our leisure is to waste our time on true philosophy.

IV.

The human intellect is defined as that faculty by which we

are capable of knowing all things, *all that is*. It has its own proper activity as well as the activity of ruling the other things in us over which it has some control – our passions, our money, our relationships. But does the intellect, as such, have a purpose other than this activity of ruling our passions or relationships? Or put it another way, what is this activity, the exercise of which gives us the intense pleasure of knowing? We do not want to know the knowing, but to know what is not ourselves. Indeed, we cannot even know ourselves unless we are in the very act of knowing something that is not ourselves. In this sense, what is not ourselves gives us ourselves to know. We know reflectively, that is, we never look directly at our own knowing but indirectly we are aware of the fact that it is we ourselves who are knowing what is not ourselves. In one sense, this is why it is all right to be a finite human being.

What is the very best thing, I ask in conclusion, that can happen to a young man or woman during his years in college? Earning a degree? I doubt it. The very best thing that can happen to us is, as Socrates put it in *The Apology*, "to know that we do not know." And this knowing that we do not know is a very active kind of a thing, it is something that wakes us up, gives us a thirst, as it were, for being, for *what is*. E. F. Schumacher, a young German, studied at Oxford in the late 1940s. He tells us in his *A Guide for the Perplexed*, of his sudden realization that in what was probably the most famous university in the world, few of the really important things were discussed. "All through school and university I had been given maps of life and knowledge on which there was hardly a trace of many of the things that I most cared about and that seemed to me to be of the greatest possible importance to the conduct of my life."[4] We are not educated simply by earning a degree. We may indeed have to learn most of the important things

4 E. F. Schumacher, *A Guide for the Perplexed* (New York: Harper Colophon, 1977), 1.

by ourselves, though even here we need help, which is why, among other things, we learn to read – read seriously, but with pleasure.

Let me conclude with two examples, one from my own experience, one from Augustine. When Augustine was about nineteen years old, as he tells us in his *Confessions*, he was a normal, bright, dissolute young man. He lived near the ancient city of Carthage. Somehow, he came across a dialogue of the Roman philosopher, Cicero, called the "Hortensius." This dialogue is now lost. But on reading it, Augustine was so inflamed with the desire to be a philosopher that he gave up all else to pursue this goal. It would be difficult to exaggerate what a momentous turning in the history of the world happened when the young Augustine read a book and decided to pursue the highest things.

When I was nineteen, by no means of the stature of the young Augustine, about whom at the time I had never heard, I was in the army at Fort Belvoir. The war was just over, so we had in fact pretty soft duty, with lots of time on our hands. We spent much of it, as young soldiers often do, in sports, drinking, and running around. But somehow, I knew that there were things that I should read. I recall going into the post library, no doubt a modest library, but still an organized library. What I remember of this scene, and what I want to leave with you, is that I looked over this library, with its ordered shelves with the usual divisions of history, novels, science, literature, religion, and philosophy, and I did not know what to read. There is no more important experience a young man or woman can have than this vivid realization that they do not know what to read.

Samuel Johnson asked, in the passage I cited in the beginning, "What say you of the peacock's tail?" I will leave you with this thought – there are things that we ought to know for their own sake, just because they are delightful, just because they are true. The peacock's tail could fan him equally efficiently or attract his mate if it were not beautiful. Aphorism #73A in Nietzsche's *Beyond Good and Evil* reads, "Many a peacock hides his peacock tail from all eyes – and calls it his pride."[5] Such pride destroys the whole point of beauty – *quod visum, placet*. Why indeed are things beautiful, things that have no other purpose but to be beautiful? This, as we will see further in the following chapter, is what leisure is about.

---

5 Friedrich Nietzsche, *Beyond Good and Evil*, trans. R. Hollingdale (Harmondsworth: Penguin, 1972), 73.

Chapter XI

LEISURE AND CULTURE
Why Human Things Exist and
Why They Are "Unimportant"

*"What benefactor has enabled you to look out
upon the beauty of the sky, the sun in its course,
the circle of the moon, the countless number of
stars, with the harmony and order that are theirs,
like the music of a harp? Who has blessed you
with rain, with the art of husbandry, with
different kinds of food, with the arts, with houses,
with laws, with states, with a life of humanity
and culture, with friendship and the easy
familiarity of kinship?"*

– St. Gregory of Nazianzen, Oratio 14,
De Pauperum Amore[1]

*"Real civilization cannot exist in the absence of a
certain play-element, for civilization presupposes
limitation and mastery of the self, the ability not
to confuse its own tendencies with the ultimate
and highest goal, but to understand that it is
enclosed within certain bounds freely accepted.
Civilization will, in a sense, always be played*

---

1 Saint Gregory of Nazianzen, "Oratio 14, *De Pauperum Amore*,"
Roman Breviary, Second Reading, Monday, First Week of Lent.

> *according to certain rules, and true civilization
> will always demand fair play. Fair play is
> nothing less than good faith expressed in play
> terms . . . To be a sound culture-creating force this
> play-element must be pure."*
>
> *– Johan Huzinga,* Homo Ludens[2]

I.

In each of these reflective citations that begin this chapter, we are admonished to do things that seem utterly useless, things not necessarily senseless, but still impractical. Beholding the beauty of the sky or counting, as Gregory calls them, the "countless stars," is really not good for much. No doubt, it can prod us to wonder why things are in this way, in this order, rather than some other arrangement. It might even impel us to send up a few space ships to have a look about. Yet, Gregory obviously thinks that what we gain from this contemplation of the heavens is well worth our efforts. And what's this about civilization "always presupposing limitation and the mastery of self"? Surely Huizinga is being ironic?

Yet, the things of civilization are also mentioned – art, houses, harps, food, laws, and "the life of humanity and culture." Gregory understands that these latter things, except for the rain, have a human component. But we still should wonder why we are said to be "blessed" with such humanlyfashioned things, almost as if they were "intended" for us to bring forth. They obviously refer us to a source not ourselves. We realize, at least implicitly, that we did not cause ourselves to be, to stand outside of nothingness. If cultural artifacts exist in some abundance, still they had to be brought forth by a being who had the capacity to create or develop them. But we did not give to ourselves this

2　Johan Huizinga, *Homo Ludens: A Study of the Play-Element in Culture* (Boston: Beacon Press [1930], 1955), 211.

artistic or craft capacity to make or order things, any more than we created the beauty of the heavens or the countless stars.

In order that something higher might be achieved among us than just our essential being, we need to act. Rules and limitations, as Huizinga paradoxically tells us, therefore, need themselves to be discovered, formulated, and, more importantly, "freely accepted." So our limitation and our freedom are not necessarily and always at logger-heads, as we are sometimes told. We need one for the other. Our freedom is directed to *what is*; we do not make or cre-ate either reality or our capacity of free will. To make a choice to have this thing is simultaneously to make a choice not to have that thing. We are only free to play the game if we agree to abide by its rules which limit us to play in the way the game is played. Otherwise, with no rules freely accepted, it is not a game and no one will play with us on any other terms. What the game is, its truth, limits our freedom to play it, that is, makes us free to play it because we accept the rules.

What is implied here is that our human life in the uni-verse reveals something of this same structure, of knowing what we are, of learning the measure or rules of our being, of freely accepting them in order that we might be what we are intended to be, human beings, not toads or gods. We seem, by being what we are, as Plato taught us, to be ordered to "play" or to participate in some transcendent game or design whose rules we do not ourselves fashion.[3] Huizinga also observes that civilization itself requires a sense of limit and self-mastery. We cannot play a game while changing its rules in the midst of the playing. We cannot create a human culture while changing the struc-ture of what it is to be human. "Man does not make him-

---

3 See James V. Schall, *Far Too Easily Pleased: A Theology of Play, Contemplation, and Festivity* (Los Angeles: Benziger/Macmillan, 1976).

self to be man," as Aristotle told us. He is already man, not of his own making. This fact itself is cause, in our souls, of the most curious of self-reflection. What is the ground of our being if we are not? The very faculty by which we consider what we are is already present in us, almost as if to say that we are meant to reflect on how we could ever come to exist since we did not cause the sorts of beings we are to come to be in the first place.

II.

Why do things exist rather than *not* exist? If precisely "nothing," in the most literal sense of the word, ever once, as it were, "existed," no thing would still "exist." *Ex nihilo, nihil fit* – a most basic of first principles of being. Why, among the vast diversity of things that do exist, are there also human things, clearly different from non-human things both above us and below us on the scale of being? Why does the existence of human things include the capacity to know the other things *that are*? Why can we only know ourselves by first knowing something that is not ourselves? And are these things that exist, human and non-human things, "important?" Important to whom? To what? For what?

We like to agree with Aristotle that nothing is made "in vain," especially ourselves. Yet, who or what might "need" us, or at least want us to be? Leisure and culture are the conditions and circumstances in which we try to respond to such questions. These are the things we do when, as I like to put it, all else is done. Our lives are not, and cannot be, exhausted in the necessary. Our being is not intended merely to keep us in existence as if just living were our highest good. We know the purpose of a doctor when we are sick, namely, to restore us to health. But what if we are "healthy"? What are the activities of health that fill our days? Surely they do not consist merely in efforts to keep us alive. We would like to know the answers to questions about *what is* just because we would like to know, just because knowing itself is a delight.

At first sight at least, such sophisticated-sounding notions as leisure and culture seem relatively insignificant compared to making and acquiring the basic necessities of life – food, clothing, shelter, economics, the production of things, war, trade. We are incessantly being urged by our churches, by our voluntary agencies, by our media to concern ourselves with the needy and the poor of various sorts. We sometimes wonder if this latter concern is not itself an escape from or avoidance of more fundamental questions. With so many things wrong or lacking in the world, in any case, why on earth, of all things, are we to be worried about "culture" and "leisure"?

Is not this leisure something we cannot "afford"? And "culture" comes from *cultus*, the notion that the highest things arise from ritual worship of the gods. Could anything be more fanciful? This same accusation, of course, was that which used to be leveled at believers by Epicureans, Marxists, and sundry militant atheists. The concern for the highest things, it was charged with some urgency, deflected us from those things that must be done for the good of the world. Culture, religion, leisure, worship were luxuries we cannot afford. It is because of them, it was charged, that the more "basic" things were neglected.

Yet, there are those, myself included, who suspect that if we do not concern ourselves with things that are not "necessary," not "important," we will never really get to those things that are commonly thought to be necessary in a worldly sense. "Seek ye first the Kingdom of God, and all these things will be added unto you." At first sight, such an admonition, even with its scriptural authority, seems absurd. It advocates the wrong priority. If we first produce "all these things" by ourselves, we then can worry about the highest things in good time. They might be nice, but we can get along fine without them. Surely we can only worry about the Kingdom of God after we have enough material things. Then we can waste time on such fanciful questions for which no one has any clear answers anyhow.

Nonetheless, Aristotle himself did tell us, in a famous passage I often cite, not to follow "those who advise us, being men, to think of human things, and, being mortal, of mortal things, but [we] must, so far as we can, make ourselves immortal, and strain every nerve to live in accordance with the best thing in us; for even if it be small in bulk, much more does it in power and worth surpass everything" (1177b31–78a2). Human things are political and economic things. While not to be neglected, they are not of highest importance. We must "strain" ourselves to seek the highest things. Aristotle clearly thinks that we can miss knowing what is important by concentrating merely on what we are in this world and its mortal activities.

We cannot, however, forget that haunting passage in *The Brothers Karamazov* in which we are warned that ultimately men would prefer bread to freedom. "For the mystery of man's being," we read in Dostoevsky, "is not only in living, but in what one lives for. Without a firm idea of what he lives for, man will not consent to live and will sooner destroy himself than remain on earth, even if there is bread all around him." Such are indeed somber, yet also hopeful, words in these days of rapid population decline in Europe and America, the effects of the culture of death. But these words remain apt commentary on the notion that man does not live by bread alone, a remark addressed to, of all people, the devil himself by Christ in the desert. The man who lives "by bread alone" is the man who lacks both culture and leisure.

To entitle, as I have, a book, *On the Unseriousness of Human Affairs*, leaves one open to certain obvious charges of denigrating the ordinary affairs of men, affairs most people take to be precisely "serious," the ones on which they spend the most time. While both accepting the validity of the point being made, the first two reviews that I saw of this book, both written fairly soon after September 11, 2001, mentioned in fact the paradox of a book suggesting that human affairs were "unserious" over against the obvious dangers and perils of a new war and numerous signs of cultural decay. The book was written before September 11, though it was not actually brought out until December of 2001. In the meantime, I had written a number of hawkish analyses of the current war against "terrorism," as it is called, the general outlines of which I approved. I likewise agree that many signs exist of – again to use that pressing word – "serious" civil decay, signs from rapid loss of population in the West, to the disorders in the family, to the legal reversal of many former sins so that they become "rights."

III.

But, to put things in perspective, I had come across C. S. Lewis's famous lecture "Learning in Wartime," given at Oxford in October of 1939, in which he said,

> The war creates no absolutely new situation. It simply aggravates the permanent human situation so that we can no longer ignore it. Human life has always been lived on the edge of a precipice. Human culture has always had to exist under the shadow of something infinitely more important than itself. If men had postponed the search for knowledge until they were secure, the search would never have begun. We are mistaken when we compare war with "normal life." Life has never been normal.[4]

From an eternal point of view, there seems to be little evidence that fewer love God in wartime than in peacetime. In fact, Scripture itself seems to suggest that, in many ways, that times of prosperity and riches are more morally dangerous than times of want and poverty. Nothing suggests that the poor of this world reach eternal life proportionally less frequently than the rich. The old monastic literature seemed to be more concerned about the souls of monks in

4 C. S. Lewis, "Learning in Wartime," *The Weight of Glory and Other Addresses* (New York: Macmillan, 1980), 21–22.

times of peace than in times of trial. Our sociological surveys likewise tell us that breakdowns in families, in society, in morality are much deeper in times of civilization and peace than in times of war when we are more likely to call upon the Lord, or at least see the need of some duty and honor.

But what about this notion of the "unseriousness of human affairs"? As I remind my friends, this title has a classical reference that any cultivated person should immediately recognize. It comes from a passage in the Seventh Book of Plato's *Laws*. The context is one that is essential for us to understand. Plato does not think that political and economic affairs are worth nothing. He grants then "a certain importance." He is aware that much of our time and energy is spent on them. But he asks of their relative importance not in light of themselves but in light of something more fascinating and absorbing. If we realize that Plato tells us what is in fact "serious," we will better understand what he means when he tells us that our human affairs are "unserious." What is serious, of course, is God.

Yet, in Plato there is nothing of the idea of "obligation" or "duty," as we often think of our relation to God. Everything is rather a spontaneous reaction to the beholding of what is beautiful. The Commandments themselves of course tell us to keep holy the Sabbath Day. They identify the Lord, our God. But revelation does not replace Plato's main point here; rather it reinforces it. If we are admonished to keep holy the Sabbath or not to take the name of the Lord in vain, we are not to think that obeying such admonitions is the essence of what revelation is telling us. We human beings are easily distracted, both to ourselves, and to our own affairs.

The first three Commandments of the Decalogue point not to ourselves, but to God. And our relation to God, as Plato intimated, is one rather closer to play than to work. It is one of those things that are "for its own sake" and not for anything we might receive. Josef Pieper put it well in his classic book, *Leisure, the Basis of Culture*: "And as it is written in the Scripture, God saw, when 'he rested from all the works that He had made' that everything was good, very good (*Genesis* 1:31), just so the leisure of man includes within itself a celebratory, approving, lingering, gaze of the inner eye on the reality of creation."[5] Not only does God delight in His creation, but His creation is to delight in what exists. Human sin, in this sense, might well be called the "disappointment of God" in the creatures not delighting both in God and in what He has made.

The point that we are to respond both to creation and to God not after the manner of need but of true delight is a delicate one. It is bound up with the very idea that God is complete in Himself, that He need not create anything, that if anything besides God does exist, it does not change God. We exist then not out of a need God had for anything, as if He lacked something, but out of His superabundance. And if God alone is "serious," it can only mean that He does not lack anything including our praise or worship. Yet, this is why we exist. We are the creatures who exist to acknowledge in the universe the glory of God in itself, for its own sake. The completion of the universe in some sense includes this chance that the free creature will recognize what is not himself, will recognize God and respond to Him simply because of *what He is*

The difference between ourselves and Plato is largely due to the fact that, with revelation, we have been given the proper way to express an appropriate worship of God. This is what the Mass is all about. It is that worship for its own sake because of the Incarnate God who offers this Sacrifice in our name, in our presence. Moreover, the word "serious" when applied to God does not imply a lack of delight and joy. It is in fact to be surrounded by music and

---

5   Josef Pieper, *Leisure: The Basis of Culture* (South Bend, Ind.: St. Augustine's Press, 1998), 133.

song. But also it implies an accurate knowledge of God. Our worship has and must have an intellectual component. This is why the Church insists that we recite the Creed each Sunday, the Creed which begins *"Credo in unum Deum. . ."* "I believe."

IV.

The two words "leisure" and "culture" have curious meanings and origins. There is a famous discussion in Aristotle about health and the activities of health. He asks, in effect, what is the difference between what a doctor does and what a healthy man does? The point can be made indirectly. When a man is not healthy, he sees the doctor to help him become healthy. The doctor does not decide what it is to be healthy. But beginning from not being healthy, he decides how to restore us to health. Once we are restored to health, we have no desire or need to see the doctor, ever again. So the activity of the doctor has a natural limit or purpose, namely, what it is to be healthy, something the doctor does not constitute but only serves. If a doctor wonders about whether he should aid us in becoming healthy, he ceases to be ruled by the end of medicine and becomes a danger to all of us.

But once I am healthy, what do I do? What are the "activities" of health? We can only answer such a question by knowing what we are. The specialist in what to do once we are healthy is not the doctor. True, we can exercise, diet, brush our teeth daily in order to remain healthy, but these are not the activities of health. In short, all those activities or professions that are primarily geared to keeping us healthy or worthy as they are, are not what we are for. I revert back to the word "strain" that Aristotle used when he told us to use every faculty we had to know as much as we could about the highest things, about *what is*, even if it be little.

What is leisure about? Essentially, it is about knowing, and knowing the truth, "to know of *what is* that it is, and

of what is not, that it is not," to cite Plato. In an old
Peanuts, We see Charlie on the mound. He is earnestly
looking at Lucy wearing what looks like an oversized baseball cap. She tells him, "Does this look all right? I've got the
ball under my cap. I'm pulling the old hidden ball trick!" As
Lucy walks away, we see Charlie on the mound yelling at
Lucy who has a frown on her face, "How are we going to
start the game if you have the ball under your cap?" In the
final scene, Lucy turns around angrily to holler back at
Charlie, "Do I have to think of everything?"[6] I suppose the
proper answer to this exasperated question of Lucy is, "No,
but you can think of anything." This is precisely the
Aristotelian definition of intellect: the capacity to know all
things, to know *what is*. But it is not necessary that we
think of everything, but we can, we have the capacity to do
so. What we lack is time and opportunity – which just may
be why we are given eternal life. "Thinking of everything,"
especially the highest things, is precisely what we are
about, even in this world.

But we are not just "thinking machines," not just dis-
embodied spirits. Every truth can have a reflection in our
world, in this world within our own minds. We often forget
that there is a pleasure also in just knowing, for no other
reason than that we want to know something, to know its
truth. We are indeed the lowest of the spiritual beings; we
have to know first by knowing through material things.
But we do know this way. And out knowing of things not
ourselves is part of the "redemption," as it were, of those
things that have no intelligence, and even more so of those
that do. We want to know most of all other persons, other
spiritual beings precisely in their inner souls. We have a
suspicion that we do not fully "exist" until we too are fully
"known."

Thus if our affairs are "unserious," if God could do with-

6 Charles Schulz, *Don't Be Sad, Flying Ace* (New York: Topper Books,
   1990).

out us, how do we go about thinking of those dire threats against living improperly that seem to come from revelation itself? Indeed, they even come from Plato. God, if I might put it that way, seems to be in the situation of someone trying to enable or encourage someone to enjoy the very best thing possible or even imaginable. But no matter what He does, the other person will not accept what is offered. And the only way the latter can have this gift is if he freely accept it. Chesterton wrote in *Orthodoxy*,

> to a Christian existence is a story, which may end up in any way. In a thrilling novel (that purely Christian product) the hero is not eaten by cannibals; but it is essential to the existence of the thrill that he might be eaten by cannibals. The hero must (so to speak) be an eatable hero. So Christian morals have always said to the man, not that he would lose his soul, but that he must take care that he didn't. In Christian morals, in short, it is wicked to call a man "damned": but it is strictly religious and philosophic to call him damnable.[7]

However we construe it, and adventure it is, if we refuse the gift that is offered freely to us, we must live with that refusal. And in this case, God could not give us His life unless we freely chose it. There is no *datur tertium*, no way to accept what it is unwillingly.

Yet, even our taking ourselves seriously is suffused with laughter. I once came across the following item in a book called *Poor H. Allen Smith's Almanac*. John XXIII is reported to have said that "it often happens that I wake at night and begin to think about a serious problem and decide I must tell the Pope about it. Then I wake up com-

7   G. K. Chesterton, *Orthodoxy* (Garden City, N.Y.: Doubleday Image, 1959), 136.

8   *Poor H. Allen Smith's Almanac: A Comic Compendium Loaded with Wisdom & Laughter, together with a Generous Lagniappe of Questionable Natural History, All Done Up in Style* (Greenwich, Conn.: Fawcett, 1965), 21

pletely and remember that I am the Pope."[8] We would be in a terrible fix, I suspect, if our popes did not have some sense of the unseriousness of even their serious lives.

The subtitle of these reflections is "why human things exist? and why they are 'unimportant.'" Human things exist but not of their own making. The cultural things that are of human making presuppose beings that did not make themselves. Human beings exist out of a superabundance of God who need not have created them. They are thus "unimportant" in comparison to their cause. But they are precisely human beings. This means they are beings with hands, passions, brains, and free wills. God deals with them according to what they are.

If I give a gift to someone I love, I do not want that gift to command or coerce the elation of the receiver. Rather, I want the receiver really to delight in the gift and in the fact that I gave it. Joy is the delight in having what we love. Our unimportance in once sense means that we take a chance in our givings. We do not know what someone will make of our beautiful gift, and a part of ourselves. It means nothing to us, but disappointment, if we receive back an artificial or strained thanks. We want the thanks to be really from the freedom and understanding, from the being of our love.

If we say that we want to know certain things not for our sakes but "for their own sakes," it means that we can actually behold the existence and beauty of something, respond to it because we really know what it is. Paradoxically, in the background of this consideration is Augustine's reminder that we are made for God from the beginning and that we cannot cease until we discover the rest for which we were intended. Yet, this is said not to depreciate or minimize the beauty of the things that are not God.

Cultus and *skole*, culture and leisure, mean that we accomplish the highest purpose in creation not in necessity or in obligation, but in delight and freedom. What we really want is what is given to us. God, for his own part, does not want our praise because He commands it. He wants it because we see that what God is, is indeed lovely, worth our awe. What we create in our human way, in our leisure and culture, ought primarily to arise out of this initial realization. The world is only complete when finite beauty is the free response to divine beauty. Only God is "serious," Plato told us. All else is "unserious." But the seriousness that is God can only mean that He prefers that we love Him for His own sake, for the sake of His beauty, because we "see" it, delight in it, after the manner in which it is given to us, as a grace which we can chose not to accept. Without this possibility of refusal, there would be no adventure, human or divine. This "refusal" will become clearer to us through Chesterton's insightful ventures into Hell and heresies in which, as in the alternative world, we can see best what we are by seeing clearly what we ought not to be.

Chapter XII

"HALOES EVEN IN HELL": CHESTERTON'S OWN PRIVATE "HERESY"

"Philosophy is merely thought that has been thought out. . . . What do modern men say when apparently confronted with something that cannot . . . be naturally explained? Well, most modern men . . . talk nonsense. When such a thing is currently mentioned, in novels or newspapers or magazine stories, the first comment is . . . something like, 'But, my dear fellow, this is the twentieth century.' It is worth having a little training in philosophy if only to avoid looking so ghastly a fool as that. It has on the whole rather less sense or meaning than saying, 'But, my dear fellow, this is Tuesday afternoon.' If miracles cannot happen, they cannot happen in the twentieth century or in the twelfth. If they can happen, nobody can prove that there is a time when they cannot happen."

– G. K. Chesterton, "The Revival of Philosophy – Why?"[1]

"When I fancied that I stood alone, I was really in the ridiculous position of being backed up by all

---

1 G. K. Chesterton, "The Revival of Philosophy – Why?" *The Common Man* (New York: Sheed & Ward, 1950), 177.

Christendom. It may be, heaven forgive me, that I did try to be original; but I only succeeded in inventing all by myself an inferior copy of the existing traditions of civilized religion. The man from the Yacht thought he was the first to find England; I thought I was the first to find Europe. I did try to found a heresy of my own; and when I had put the last touches to it, I discovered that it was orthodoxy."

– *G. K. Chesterton,* Orthodoxy[2]

"I have much more sympathy for the person who leaves the Church for a love-affair than with one who leaves it for a long-winded German theory to prove that God is evil or that children are a sort of morbid monkey."

– *G. K. Chesterton,* Catholic Church and Conversion[3]

I.

In this penultimate chapter, I propose that most of the things we have been considering thus far can be seen reflected in the English writer G. K. Chesterton's own delightful account of how he discovered sanity, *what is*. In the first chapter of his *Autobiography*, appropriately entitled, "Hearsay Evidence," thus chiding modern scientific method, Chesterton candidly admits to having no personal proof of his own first appearance on earth. Rather, he confesses, he must rely entirely on "mere authority and tradition of the elders," which does, however quite illogically, to be sure, leave him with the "firm opinion" that he was "born on the 29th of May 1874, on Campden Hill, Kensington."[4]

2 G. K. Chesterton, *Orthodoxy, Collected Works* (San Francisco: Ignatius, [1908] 1986), I, 214. Italics added.

3 G. K. Chesterton, *Catholic Church and Conversion, General Works* (San Francisco: Ignatius Press, [1927] 1990), III, 123.

4 G. K. Chesterton, *The Autobiography, Collected Works* (San Francisco: Ignatius Press, [1936] 1988), XVI, 21.

In this chapter, Chesterton speaks of his maternal grandfather, "a Keith from Aberdeen," a Scotsman, a Wesleyan lay-preacher. Chesterton never saw this grandfather but had memorable images of him from his grandmother, a "vivid personality," who long survived her husband. Chesterton saw something of himself in this grandfather. He "was involved in public controversy, a characteristic which descended to his grandchild." Chesterton adds, however, that "he was also one of the leaders of the early Teetotal movement; a characteristic which has not" so descended to his grandchild.[5]

Chesterton recalls hearing of a controversy between this Scot grandfather and his sons about "the General Thanksgiving in the Prayer-Book." One of them remarked that "a good many people have very little reason to be thankful for their creation." On hearing this pessimistic comment, the old man, "who was so old that he hardly ever spoke at all," suddenly came to life and out of his silence affirmed, "I should thank God for my creation if I knew I was a lost soul."[6] Lost souls even in Hell, perhaps they above all, know that creation is good in spite of themselves; otherwise there would be no point to be in Hell, to losing one's soul.

This paradoxical combination of gratefulness for our existence together with an awareness that we can lose our souls in a good world is the inheritance that Chesterton received from a grandfather Keith in Aberdeen, to pass on to us. That we receive such truths third-hand from two figures we have never seen does not make such insights less wondrous or less true. How should we react to such unexpected, even slightly unorthodox sounding, insight from, what must be in the modern world, an improbable source stemming from Aberdeen to Campden Hill, Kensington, in 1874, and finally to us in the the twenty-first century?

5 Ibid., 29.
6 Ibid., 29–30.

One July, I received an unanticipated e-mail from a student from one of my past classes who told me that she was not from Cincinnati, as I had thought, but "from a charming little beach town in Rhode Island." I had sent her a brief passage from Chesterton, I forget now what. She replied, "I am actually reading *Orthodoxy* right now. I can only say that I am enchanted." This is the perfect word about Chesterton, isn't it? "Enchantment." As I shall suggest, even when he talks of "lost souls," or "heresies," or "Hell," or "pride" or "Original Sin," there remains a certain enchantment about Chesterton, a wonder that can see the order of things even in things that are completely disordered. Through his eyes, we see again in a new light everything we have thus far seen.

II.

The most ironic of paradoxes would be to maintain, as I do maintain, that Chesterton himself was the ultimate "heretic," the one who did reject the prevailing intellectual fashions of his day in order to formulate his own private "heresy." He was the one man who was not saying what everyone else was saying. How so? The ultimate heretic in a fallen world would be someone who, in the end, was so odd, so "illogical," so contrary to prevailing propositions as to find that an "order" did run through all the philosophical and religious systems, especially in those systems that maintain that there is no order or system.

This order in disorder, as it unravels itself, is found by examining the positions that men hold or claim that they hold about both ordinary and ultimate things. The raw material from which we begin is not belief, but prevailing opinion, the opinion which attempts to explain things, the opinion that underlies and presumably justifies our actions.

The method presupposes, of course, the validity of the principle of contradiction. That is, it holds that something cannot be and not be at the same time and in the same circumstances. On the validity of this principle, which to deny is likewise to affirm, depends all human discourse, indeed human existence. Chesterton, if you will, was delighted by contradictions wherever they were found, for they hinted that not all was contradictory, that something was in fact true and stable.

Let us suppose, for example, that the principle of contradiction is *not* true, that a thing can be and not be at the same time, in the same way. Let us suppose, furthermore, that someone stands before me and affirms that he exists, or even that I exist. Since, in this hypothesis, the principle of contradiction is not true, I have no idea whether the man is really there in front of me, since he can "not be" at the same time that he is. The denial of the principle does not allow me to distinguish his existence from his non-existence. Nor can I be sure that he affirms anything at all. His affirming that he is standing before me could be likewise a not-affirming that he stands before me. Indeed, on the same hypothesis, I cannot even be sure that I exist or that I have a mind bothered by any principles whatsoever.

Chesterton, as he tells us, does not arrive at the frontiers of Christianity though some vibrant preacher, even his Wesleyan grandfather. He did not read his way into the Church through a philosopher, say, Newman or Augustine or even Aquinas, each of whom he admired. He was not present at some miracle that compelled his soul. Nor was he, like St. Paul, knocked off a horse after a busy spell of persecuting hapless Christians. Chesterton does not seem to have been a Bible reader. He was convinced that rather few Protestants in his time believed the exact same doctrines that the founders of Protestantism held. He was not willing to take any Protestant position seriously until it took itself seriously. "There are Catholics who are still answering Calvinists," he remarked, "though there are no Calvinists to answer."[7]

7 *Catholic Church and Conversion*, ibid., 41. "The genuine Protestant creed is now hardly held by anybody – least of all by the Protestants.

Chesterton tells us himself that he mainly read modern thinkers, writers, apologists, scientists, historians, philosophers, theologians. In his early book, *Heretics*, he called his intellectual contemporaries, using the word in its broad philosophical and theological sense, precisely "heretics." Much of what he learned, he read in the papers. In fact, he considered the daily newspapers, for which he indeed wrote all his life, to be stocked full of reality, especially the actual vagaries and varieties of the human condition. They at least were real, but needed sorting out.

Reading such sundry sources, Chesterton came to a sudden realization. One way of putting the matter was contained in this famous line: "The Catholic Church is the only thing which saves a man from the degrading slavery of being a child of his age."[8] He found that the thinkers of his age often contradicted themselves, especially on important issues, because they had no standard against which to compare what they came to hold. One writer would say one thing of some topic and another would maintain just the opposite, or the same man would hold one thing one decade and another the next without ever noticing the difference. Both positions could not be true. This was "multi-culturalism" before its official appearance.

III.

As time went on, what Chesterton found even more curious was that the most egregious contradictions appeared to have something to do with describing Christianity and the

So completely have they lost faith in it, that they have mostly forgotten what it was. If almost any modern man be asked whether we save our souls solely thorough our theology, or whether doing good (to the poor for instance) will help us on the road to God, he would answer without hesitation that good works are probably more pleasing to God than theology. It would probably come as quite a surprise to him to learn that, for three hundred years, the faith in faith alone was the badge of a Protestant, the faith in good works the rather shameful badge of a disreputable Papist." G. K. Chesterton, *The Thing: Why I Am a Catholic* (San Francisco: Ignatius Press, 1990), III, 185–86.

8 *Catholic Church and Conversion*, ibid., 110.

Church, what it held and why it did what it did. He was
puzzled by this array of contradictory charges and affirmations made against Catholics. It might be true that Christ
performed miracles. It might be true that He did not. But
it could not be true that He both did and did not. Christ, for
example, was said by some critics to be too harsh, by others too gentle. Too tall or too short. Some thought He was
only man, others that He was only God. All seemed to have
had before them the same evidence about the same person.

Gradually, it dawned on Chesterton that Christ could
not be all these things at once. The mind would not allow
it. He could not be too tall and too short at the same time.
But, Chesterton reflected, if He were pretty normal, more
or less average, then to those who were short, He would
look tall. To the tall, he would look short. Strange as it may
seem, the reason why all these differing estimates made
sense was that He was pretty much what He said He was.
He could not be explained by making Him either God or
man, but by acknowledging that He was both. Chesterton
was astonished that it was precisely the Creeds that made
this acknowledgment.

In seeking to understand the logic behind such contradictions, Chesterton discovered an alternative that made
sense. His mind could not rest content with contradictions,
but contradictions pointed to the truth. To himself,
Chesterton seemed to be odd man out. He was the
"heretic"; he was the one who said something really different, not just that Christianity was true, but that it was
reasonable in its truth. "Amid all these anti-rational
philosophies, ours will remain the only rational philosophy," he wrote.[9] As he admitted later, he admired tough-
ness of mind. "A convinced Catholic is easily the most hard-
headed and logical person walking about the world
today."[10] Notice that Chesterton does not appeal to revela-

9　Ibid., 68.
10 *The Thing*, ibid., 286.

tion in the name of revelation, but to revelation in the name of reason. He makes his case almost as if to say that revelation is itself addressed to reason, which indeed it is.

Chesterton was not "converted" by Christians to Christianity. He was converted to Christianity by heretics and non-believers explaining, often to themselves, what they held, especially what they held about Christianity. "Here I am only giving an account of my own growth in spiritual certainty," Chesterton wrote near the end of *Orthodoxy*. "But I may pause to remark that the more I saw of the merely abstract arguments against the Christian cosmology the less I thought of them. I mean that having found the moral atmosphere of the Incarnation to be common sense, I then looked at the established intellectual arguments against the Incarnation and found them to be common nonsense."[11] Notice that here that Chesterton is not using reason to "prove" the fact of the Incarnation – that would indeed be "heresy" – rather he is using reason to examine the arguments proposed against the Incarnation, itself something revealed to us. These counter-arguments were, as he quips, generally found to be "common nonsense."

Chesterton gained a further insight into what goes on in such intellectual analysis by following the drift of those who think that they do have adequate arguments against Christianity. Chesterton's life, of course, was filled with happy argument. He thrived on it and, such was the pleasantness of his character, even those who were subject to his witty and often devastating criticisms, seemed still to love him. He delighted in controversy and thought that the brain was given to us so that we could arrive at the truth through argument. Moreover, he thought we should express this truth precisely in dogmas, in clear statements we can examine, even when they referred to the highest mysteries which no purely human mind could completely comprehend.

11 *Orthodoxy*, ibid., 347.

Chesterton remarked in his book on St. Thomas that the trouble with most arguments is that they are unfair, because they end too soon, before the logical consequences can be drawn out of them. He hinted that this very unfairness was often part of a strategy to prevent the truth from being confronted. The other side of this concern about long arguments is related to why Chesterton loved camaraderie and long nights of drink and discussion in local pubs when there would be time to see just where argument really went, when no one would be allowed to hide behind a rank contradiction without knowing it is a rank contradiction.

But something even more sinister seemed to be at work here. "This is the last and most astounding fact about this faith," Chesterton wrote, again in *Orthodoxy*, "that its [Christianity's] enemies will use any weapon against it, the swords that cut their own fingers, and the firebrands that burn their own homes. Men who began to fight the Church for the sake of freedom and humanity, end up by flinging away freedom and humanity if only they may fight the Church."[12] This passage indicates just why it is important to have, in the Church itself, intelligence, to notice precisely that point when an objection is answered but a movement against truth goes on in bad faith either because it does not want to admit its error or because it does not want to live the truth. It is from this source that discrimination and even persecution originates. The world, alas, does not only contain "errors." It also contains "bad will." This combination of error and bad will also requires philosophical explication, an explication rooted in the very nature of will.

IV.

Let me take two basic instances wherein Chesterton tells of discovering his own religion only to find it a) contrary to

12 Ibid., 344.

what was being held in the culture at the time and b) in conformity with what Christianity historically taught. On September 18, 1920, still a few years before he became a Catholic, Chesterton wrote: "Men do not believe in Original Sin because they believe in the Book of *Genesis*. They are ready to believe in the Book of *Genesis*, because they already believe in Original Sin."[13] Chesterton often came back to the question of Original Sin or the Fall. He maintained that it was the one Christian doctrine that did not need theological proof. All we needed to do was to go out into the streets and open our eyes. Strictly speaking, this explanation is probably a "heretical" position. But Chesterton meant what Aristotle meant when he was perplexed by the "wickedness" that kept recurring in human experience and the futility with the economic, political, or religious efforts devised to eradicate it from our lot in this life. Original Sin is not intended to excuse our sins, but to locate their origins and reasons. It is intended to warn us about proposing solutions for its presence that by-pass the human soul, with its free will. The intellectual world is structured so as to allow no escape from free will to determinism.

Chesterton's understanding of Original Sin was not "morbid," but it was "realistic" in the sense of Augustinian realism, that things do go wrong, even among the faithful, perhaps especially among the faithful. Murphy's famous law, "if a thing can go wrong, it will go wrong," and the Peter Principle, that "a man rises to the level of his incompetence," are but amusing observation on some uncanny disorder in our universal experience. Original Sin, the experience of its presence in all times and cultures, points not to Utopia but to Incarnation, not to a placed where it is

13 G. K. Chesterton, "Modern Vagueness about Theology," *Illustrated London News, Collected Works* (San Francisco: Ignatius Press, 1989), 91.

"cured," but to a place where it is redeemed. Incarnation, however, points not to a this-worldly paradise but to the Resurrection of the Body. One of Chesterton's abiding themes is that we are, in fact, created for a joy that is too good to be true. The trouble with humanist alternatives is not that they are necessarily ignoble, but that they do not offer to us what we really want.

Thus, we can even find a certain "cheerfulness" about this often troubling doctrine of Original Sin. This is how Chesterton put the issue in *Orthodoxy*:

> All the real arguments about religion turn on the question of whether a man who was born upside down can tell when he comes right way up. The primary paradox of Christianity is that the ordinary condition of man is not his sane or sensible condition; that the normal self is an abnormality. That is the inmost philosophy of the Fall. In Sir Oliver Lodge's interesting new Catechism, the first two questions were: "What are you?" and "What, then, is the meaning of the Fall of Man?" I remember amusing myself by writing my own answers to the questions: but I soon found that they were broken and agnostic answers. To the question, "What are you?" I could only answer, "God knows." And to the question, "What is meant by the Fall?" I could answer with complete sincerity, "That whatever I am, I am not myself." This is the prime paradox of our religion: something that we have never in any full sense known, is not only better than ourselves, but even more natural to us than ourselves.[14]

This is a remarkable passage, well worth spelling out in some detail. We are born upside down. Our problem is to learn to recognize what is right side up.

Take for instance the question of surveys or polls designed to discover what men "do" – they steal, commit adultery, lie, kill, as it turns out. Lo and behold, we find that a certain percentage in any society – it may vary in

14 Chesterton, *Orthodoxy*, ibid., 363.

times and places – do these very things, some of which, at least, we think ought not to be done. What happens next is to discover "scientifically" that it is "normal" that we find such sins or disorders among us. Josef Pieper, in his book, *The Concept of Sin*, has an interesting chapter on how touchy we are about using the word "sin" for any of these "faults," except maybe in jest.[15] Some historic sins are now, in fact, called "rights," a fact that forces the question on us of whether human nature changes over time and place, even whether it changes so much as to approve in one generation the opposite of what it approved in a previous generation.

If we analyze all of this information carefully, however, we see Chesterton's very point. The fact that we are sinful and do sinful things – statistics prove it, whatever we call it – suggests that somehow our "normal" condition – the one most of us display – is, by another criterion, abnormal. We "do" not what we want or ought to do, to recall a famous phrase of St. Paul. The fact that a culture or society wants to call what is sinful "normal" thus does not mean that it is in fact normal. It only means that it is frequent. But by another standard we cannot avoid pondering, it may very well be "abnormal." The normal, in the sense of what is proper to human nature, is not what we actually do, but what we ought to do. "The ordinary condition of man is nor his sane or sensible condition." This seems to be exactly right. We are precisely "heretics" today if we maintain that the order of the Commandments is the order that is best for us. We conform to the culture, we are slaves to our time, if we say that what we do "do" is what is "right" for us to do.

V.

A second area in which Chesterton discovered his own

15 Josef Pieper, *The Concept of Sin* (South Bend, Ind.: St. Augustine's Press, 2001).

"religion," because of which he was a "heretic" in the culture, was in the area of marriage and what it means. Again, we live in a society in which monogamous marriage designed for a lifetime together amid one's own children is not the "norm." That is, most people do not live in such a permanent marital situation. What Chesterton wants to know, however, is "what do I really want, if I could have it?" In *What's Wrong with the World*, Chesterton remarks that most people would want a home, property, family. This is the material foundation that establishes the family in some sense free from, independent of, the state. The family is beyond law in the sense that love is beyond law.

Chesterton rejected the Platonic or socialist ideal of all men, women, and children living in common houses or messes or care institutions. "That all men should live in the same beautiful house is not a dream at all; it is a nightmare."[16] Having what is one's own is part of the adventure of the distinctness of creation itself, the fact that not all things are the same. "The perfect happiness of men on the earth (if it ever comes) will not be a flat and solid thing, like the satisfaction of animals. It will be an exact and perilous balance, like that of a desperate romance. Man must have just enough faith in himself to have adventures, and just enough doubt of himself to enjoy them."[17] Faith is the origin of joy, while humility is the source of romance

Chesterton maintained that he could found his own religion, the one in which he was and is still precisely a "heretic" to the culture, because of his understanding of love and marriage. The first thing we need to know about is that marriage is a metaphysical thing. We want someone to love who is not ourselves; that is, we want the world to be so structured that we are not the only ones in it. We want the other to be the other and to remain the other. We want, as Chesterton wrote in his book on St. Thomas, a

16 *Orthodoxy*, ibid., 327–28.
17 Ibid., 318.

metaphysics that guarantees the diversity of things. We do not want all things to be the same, even when we want them to have their fair due. "Without vanity," Chesterton wrote, "I really think there was a moment when I could have invented the marriage vow (as an institution) out of my own head; but I discovered, with a sigh, that it had been invented already."[18] Chesterton recognizes what a relief it is that we do not have to create our own world, that it may well be better made than anything that we could come up with.

What was it about the marriage vow in particular that interested Chesterton? "I do not know if the reader agrees with me in these examples; but I will add an example which has always affected me most. I could never conceive or tolerate any Utopia which did not leave to me the liberty for which I chiefly care, the liberty to bind myself. Complete anarchy would not only make it impossible to have any discipline or fidelity; it would also make it impossible to have any fun."[19] That the marriage vow also had something to do with the protection of discipline, fidelity, and fun is something that perhaps only Chesterton could have seen. One might well argue, on empirical grounds, that the violation of the vows is precisely what has caused widespread lack of discipline, lack of fidelity, and a kind of sadness among us.

There is one more thing about the marriage vow that is worth recalling. In his famous essay, "In Defense of Rash Vows," which appeared in *The Defendant* in 1901, Chesterton not only linked the vow to the notion of love and permanent friendship but also to the ever-present threat of Original Sin even in the best of marriages. A vow, after all, is a solemn promise to stay together, not merely

> when times are good, but especially when times are
> bad. "There are thrilling moments, doubtless, for the

18 Ibid., 327.
19 Ibid., 328.

spectator, the amateur, and the ascetic; but there is one thrill that is known only to the soldier who fights for his own flag, to the ascetic who starves himself for is own illumination, to the lover who makes finally how own choice. And it is this transfiguration of self-discipline that makes the vow a truly sane thing."[20]

It is the "freedom to bind oneself," as Chesterton put it. Love wants to bind and to be bound, but mutually and freely.

The revolt against vows has been carried in our day even to the extent of a revolt against the typical vow of marriage. It is most amusing to listen to the opponents of marriage on this subject. They appear to imagine that the ideal of constancy was a yoke mysteriously imposed on mankind by the devil, instead of being, as it is, a yoke consistently imposed by all lovers on themselves. They have invented a phrase, a phrase that is a black and white contradiction in two words – "free-love" – as if a lover ever had been, or ever could be, free. It is the nature of love to bind itself, and the institution of marriage merely paid the average man the compliment of taking him at his word.[21]

Chesterton thought that the adventure that marriage puts into the world, the freedom to bind oneself to someone, was "democratic," that it was open equally to the rich and the poor, the great and the ordinary. This position meant that there was drama all around us, especially if we had homes formed by this mutual binding.

VI.

At the end of *Heretics*, we find the following almost prophetic prediction about the relation of reason and reve-

20 G. K. Chesterton, "In Defence of Rash Vows," *The Defendant* (London: Dent, [1901] 1914), 26.
21 Ibid., 23.

lation, faith and philosophy. It remains one of the first and probably the last and finest statements of Chesterton about what he saw of the modern mind when left to itself. It is his statement of where the heresies that deviated from orthodoxy would ultimately lead.

> The great march of mental destruction will go on. Everything will be denied. Everything will become a creed. It is a reasonable position to deny the stones in the street; it will be a religious dogma to assert them. It is a rational thesis that we are all in a dream; it will be a mystical sanity to say that we are all awake. Fires will be kindled to testify that two and two make four. Swords will be drawn to prove that leaves are green in summer. We shall be left defending, not only the incredible virtues and sanities of human life, but something more incredible still, the huge impossible universe which stares us in the face. We shall fight for visible prodigies as if they were invisible. We shall look on the impossible grass and the skies with a strange courage. We shall be of those who have seen and yet have believed.[22]

Chesterton was right. Modern philosophy has not only doubted the order, even existence of the world, but it has doubted its own mind. It does take "courage" to affirm the grass is green and that we can know *what is*. It was Christ himself, after all, who said to the Apostle Thomas, "blessed are they Thomas who have not seen but who have believed." What Chesterton saw one hundred years ago was that it would be revelation that finally ends up defending reason and its ability to reach a real world that is not ourselves, though we are in it, yet not wholly at home in it.

In a chapter entitled, "Is Humanism a Religion," in *The Thing: Why I Am a Catholic*, the book Chesterton wrote in 1922 to explain his conversion, we find this passage, with which I shall conclude

22 G. K. Chesterton, Heretics, Collected Works (San Francisco: Ignatius Press, [1905] 1986), I, 206–7.22.

There are, as a matter of fact, any number of old pictures in which whole crowds are crowned with haloes,
to indicate that they have all attained Beatitude. But
for Catholics, it is a fundamental dogma of the Faith
that all human beings, without any exception whatever, were specially made, were shaped and pointed like
shining arrows, for the end of hitting the mark of
Beatitude. It is true that the shafts are feathered with
free will, and therefore throw the shadow of all tragic
possibilities of free will, and that the Church (having
also been aware for ages of that darker side of truth,
which the new sceptics have just discovered) does also
draw attention to the darkness of that potential
tragedy. But that does not make any difference to the
gloriousness of the potential glory. In one aspect it is
even a part of it; since the freedom is itself a glory. In
that sense they would still wear their *haloes even in
hell*.[23]

Freedom is itself a glory even for those who abuse it.
Chesterton's private "heresy" would allow "haloes in Hell"
because no glory is to be taken away from the potential
glory in which we are made, exactly made.

Chesterton's grandfather Keith would still thank God
even if he lost his soul. There are many who do not want to
face the terms of glory, the fact that we must choose it. The
ultimate "heresy," Chesterton thought, was not his invention, though he did come to a pale shadow of it by pondering the contradictions of the heretics of his time. The ultimate heresy was already in existence and Chesterton
found it. "We need so to view the world," Chesterton wrote
at the beginning of *Orthodoxy*, "as to combine the idea of
wonder and the idea of welcome."[24] These were philosophical ideas that rang true to him. What astonished him and
enchants us is that this wonder and this welcome are the

23 G. K. Chesterton, *The Thing: Why I Am a Catholic, Collected Woks*
    (San Francisco, Ignatius Press [1926] 1990), 150. Italics added.
24 *Orthodoxy*, ibid., 213.

essence of revelation.

The *haloes of Hell* and the heresies of modernity, each in their own way, attest to the fact that Chesterton had it right. "How," he asked, "can we continue to be at once astonished at the world and at home in it?"[25] Only if we accept this "ultimate heresy" that contradicts all the contradictions lodged against it. This is what happened once in our era, when an insightful man set out "to found a heresy of his own." He discovered, as we all must, the fuller meaning of happiness.

Chapter XIII

ON THE SUM TOTAL OF HUMAN HAPPINESS

"I [Boswell] mentioned that I was afraid I put into my journal too many little incidents. Johnson 'There is nothing, Sir, too little for so little a creature as man. It is by studying little things that we attain the great art *of having as little misery and as much happiness as possible.'"*
— Boswell's Life of Johnson, *1763*[1]

"The perfection of each individual thing considered in itself is imperfect, being a part of the perfection of the entire universe, which arises from the sum total of the perfections of all individual things. And so, in order that there might be some remedy for this imperfection, *another kind of perfection is to be found in created things. It consists in this: that the perfection belonging to one thing, is found in another. This is the perfection of the knower insofar as he knows. . . . Hence, as it is said in* On the Soul *III that the soul is in a certain way all things since its nature is such that it can know all things. In this way it is possible for the perfection of the*

---

1 *Boswell's Life of Johnson* (London: Oxford University Press, 1931), I, 290.

entire universe to exist in one thing. The ultimate perfection achievable by the soul, then, according to the philosophers, is to have inscribed in it the entire order and causes of the universe. And they also held that this is to be the ultimate end of man. (We, however, hold that it consists in the vision of God, for, as Gregory says, 'What is there that they do not see, who see Him Who sees all things?')"

– Thomas Aquinas, De Veritate, 2, 2

"Knowing is the creature's best chance to overcome the law of nonbeing, the wretchedness inflicted upon it by the real diversity of 'that which is' and 'to be.' A thing which is not God cannot be except at the cost of not being what it is not. It cannot be except by being deprived of indefinitely many forms and perfections. To this situation knowledge, according to St. Thomas's words, is a remedy, inasmuch as every knowing subject is able to have, over and above its own forms, the form of other things."

– Yves Simon, A General Theory of Authority[2]

I.

The most famous book that talks to us of precisely "human" happiness, the proper happiness of man in so far as he is man in this world, is, no doubt, Aristotle's *Ethics*. Here he tells us, as if looking into our own souls in our own time, that everything we do, all the particular, singular things in which our actions exist and which constitute the outlines of our lives, we do because we seek to be happy by the doing of these actions. This seeking to be happy in each particular act is what unites all the things that do exist insofar as they are touched by human minds and hands. All human beings reveal the same curious variety of longings in their origins. The world, in other words, is full of things that

2 Yves Simon, *A General Theory of Authority* (Notre Dame, Ind.: University of Notre Dame Press, [1962] 1980), 152.

came to be because someone sought to be happy and did something to attain this purpose, albeit not always the right thing or the best thing.

Aristotle next explains to us that we can have differing ideas of that in which this happiness consists, but even here, the general diversity is not so great when we come to examine it. The great variations that seem at first sight evident in human searchings can be subsumed under four general headings. Some think that happiness is money, some pleasure, some honor or power, and still others think it consists in human contemplation of truth, of knowing the things *that are.* Happiness, Aristotle tells us, is an activity, it is an activity of our highest faculties on the highest objects in a complete life, but it does not exclude any activity's worth nor does it deny the wide diversity of human things, good and bad, that occurs as a result of this seeking.

At first sight, this explanation will sound very exalted, perhaps abstract. Moreover, it seems odd, as the classical writers maintained, to claim that only a few philosophers can, in the proper sense, be happy, since most folks most of the time seem to be off pursuing money, honors, or pleasures, all good things in a way, but not the highest things. But in attributing this more perfect happiness to a few philosophers, the classical writers were merely going by what they observed. Yet, we wonder about ordinary things, the small things in the overall order of things, the things that we attribute to everyone, even philosophers, in their normal lives.

In Tolkien's *The Two Towers,* after the fellowship is broken, the dwarf Gimli complains to Aragorn, the Strider, that the Lady Galadriel had not given them the same magic light that she had given to Frodo. Aragorn replies that it is more needed by Frodo, for his is the main Quest concerning the first ring. Then Aragorn adds, "ours is but a small matter in the great deeds of this time."[3] Here, as it

3 J. R. R. Tolkien, *The Two Towers* (New York: Ace Books, 1965), 25.

were, I am concerned as much about the "small matters" as about "the great deeds." At times, I think the small matters are much more difficult to explain than the great deeds, though the central issue is how we have deeds, great or small, to explain. And though it is implied that by Aragorn that there is a difference between great things and small things, we get the distinct impression that the small things are still of great importance.

The classical reflections on happiness as our highest end seem, at first sight at least, to leave aside much of what actually happens to us, the small things, if you will. Our lives are filled with a myriad of differing activities and deeds. We see, hear, encounter many, many things, strange things. We forget how easily the familiar things once appeared to be strange to us. We tend to forget their strangeness because we have become familiar with them. Even Aristotle said that we can spend little time on the highest things, though we should spend as much time as we can on them. Many things "have" to be done that we would just as soon, if we could, avoid – from brushing our teeth to mowing our lawns to locking our houses at night. Surely, we do not want to be snobs or elitists, to develop a philosophy of only the "highest things." The Lord told us to "behold the lilies of the field, how they grow." He did not tell us to learn how to use fertilizer or how to irrigate to improve plant growth or yield. Pioneer Hybrids and de Kalb had to figure this latter out by themselves.

This encouragement to pay attention to the beauty of the simple things that grow – we could say the same of apple trees, or little kittens, as we do of the lilies of the field – seems to be part of the purpose of revelation, as if to say, in principle at least, that to miss anything on the way to knowing *all that is* turns out to be a mistake. Chesterton once remarked that "there is no such thing as an uninteresting subject; the only thing that can exist is an uninterested person."[4] He hints here that what is brought out of

4 G. K. Chesterton, *Heretics* (New York: John Lane, 1914), 38.

nothingness, just any particular thing, is itself somehow related to what can cause existence in the first place. All things are unified in this common origin. Sometimes we also hear that we should seek the *unum necessarium*, the one thing necessary, the highest thing, and we should.

But what I want to suggest here is that we should also look to and wonder about the infinity of things that are quite unnecessary, however glorious or interesting they might be. One of the most remarkable things about creation, besides the fact that it is at all, is the number of apparently unnecessary things in it, almost as if our origins are not at all in parsimony but in an abundance that we are almost loathe to admit. We can almost reverse Occam's famous razor which maintained that *entia non sunt multiplicanda nisi per necessitatem* – beings are not to be multiplied unless by necessity. The fact is, things are indeed multiplied almost as if necessity had nothing to do with it. And yet this abundance, even in its incredible particularity, seems to relate to us, to our power of knowing and appreciating. Our mind is called by Aristotle the faculty that is *capax omnium*, a definition about which we do well to reflect with great astonishment. Its very purpose or power relates us to *all that is*.

II.

The expression, "the sum total of human happiness," stands in contrast to "the sum total of human misery." We presume that one counterbalances or even overcomes the other. And we are not naive enough, unobservant enough, to deny the reality of human misery, itself something that we can know or know about, something present to us. The "great art of life," Samuel Johnson tells us, is to have as much happiness and as little misery as possible. Johnson recognizes that, very often, our happiness exists, paradoxically, in the "little" things. And even if he calls man himself "so little a creature," it is because although most lives are unknown to most of the world, still they are lives, still worth living. We are not gods; it is not our destiny to become some other kind of a being besides the specific human being that we are. It is all right, in other words, to be what we are.

In this great art of life, Johnson affirms that small happinesses count, while little miseries hurt. This observation implies that if we are not content in small things, we may likewise miss any contentment in the great ones. No life is composed only of "great things." Small things likewise lead to all things. The explanation of the existence of small things is, be it noted, as mysterious as the existence of the great things – both have their origins in *what is*. The "micro" universe is as difficult to explain as the "macro" universe, though, be it noted, we attempt to do both.

Neither happiness nor misery, moreover, can belong to anyone other than an individual person. We find many existing persons, many kinds of activities in which happiness or misery might be thought to exist. The "greatest happiness to the greatest numbers" is, at first sight, a similar and familiar phrase, yet one fraught with danger. No "greatest" collective being exists to whom we might attribute this "greatest happiness." The universe is so created that happiness is spread out into billions and billions of particular beings who can know it, seek it as properly their own. Happiness does not float around ungrounded outside of particular persons, however much they might be related to one another in justice, love, or friendship. And this "greatest happiness," by some perverse calculations, might be achieved at the expense of the misery of others who do not compose the greatest numbers. The subject that bears happiness or misery is always the individual person in whom the drama of existence is centered.

But no doubt, if we be sane, we want many, not just ourselves, to be happy. Likewise, we want few to be miserable. There is such a thing as sacrificial suffering, but it too is rooted in what, in principle, ought not to be. Yet, part of happiness is in learning how to live through our miseries, or at least to know how misery is related to happiness. In some obscure sense, our miseries also teach us about our happiness. No life will be happiness-guaranteed or misery-free. The "sum total of human happiness" must include little things as well as great things. Human happiness does not simply consist in the "great" things, however much it includes them also. Everything about human life has something of significance attached to it because *all that is* contains something of interest, something the human mind can know. The "sum total of human happiness" is directly related to the fact that all things are good, almost as if that very affirmation is a challenge for us to find it.

But the "sum total of human happiness" remains a curious expression nonetheless. Happiness, we are told by the philosophers, is an activity. Indeed it is an activity of all our capacities on their proper objects. And that about which we are active always reaches to something not ourselves. We are self-insufficient when it comes to our own happiness, as we are self-insufficient when it comes to knowing. While we might want ourselves to be happy, our happiness does not consist in only ourselves. "Man as he is constituted, endowed as he is with a thirst for happiness," Josef Pieper has written,

> cannot have his thirst quenched in the finite realm; and if he thinks or behaves as if that were possible, he is misunderstanding himself, he is acting contrary to his own nature. The whole world would not suffice this "natural" nature of man. If the whole world were given to him, he would have to say, and would say: It is too little. Too little, that is, to "gratify entirely the power of desire," or in other words, too little to make him happy.[5]

This again is the contrast between the one thing necessary and all the other things. In desiring the one thing

5 Josef Pieper, *Happiness and Contemplation*, trans. Richard and Clara Winston (New York: Pantheon, 1958; South Bend, Ind.: St. Augustine's Press, 1998), 38–39.

necessary, the highest things, we do not on that account cease to be interested in the things that in their being are not necessary. They too have a wonder.

One famous definition of hell, indeed, is that Hell is to be with ourselves alone with nothing else, forever – a terrifying thought. The highest activity ought not to be, though it can be, in opposition to the lowest activity. There is an order of things. Our being displays or calls forth a harmony of higher and lower that still must be produced in each life. This "calling forth" is indeed what constitutes the drama of each life. Whatever is proper to man belongs to him for what he is. Though there be a diversity of parts and capacities in man, still he is a one, a single being in which this diversity has an order to an end. He is a whole and as such he confronts *all that is*, all that is not himself, all indeed that is himself.

Moreover, as man discovers soon enough, each of his given and proper activities has its own pleasure that is present within the activity, both to encourage us to do the activity and to complete it. The perfection of an activity in a way includes, but is not identical with, its accompanying pleasure. In pleasure there is an abundance, and in knowledge there is a superabundance of activity. We can often, at least in intention, separate an activity's purpose from the pleasure that accompanies it. The fact that we can make this separation is one of the reasons why we can err or sin in our activities. We can argue ourselves into following the logic of pleasure and not the logic of the activity's true purpose. But it is not intended to be this way. We are not stoics who think that we must overcome all pleasure or pain in the name of duty. We are rather Aristoteleans who think that we must find the purpose of any activity and enjoy the pleasure that naturally accompanies it when it is done properly. These considerations are important if we are to approach the meaning of the sum total of human happiness.

We can postulate initially that no one will ever experience in himself the "sum total of human happiness," no matter how happy he may be. Yet, we can also postulate that every kind of activity and pleasure is presented in our being. We are a microcosmos in which all levels of being, mineral, vegetative, animal, and sprit exist in us, by nature. Nor does this approach deny the question of what is the highest happiness. Happiness is the activity of the highest faculty on the highest object in a complete life, to repeat Aristotle's definition of it. On the objective side, we need to know as best we can just what is this object to which our highest faculty is ordained. We need to have some estimate about what this object, that is not ourselves, might be. This is why we are given intellect, and with it, philosophy, the quest to know *what is*. This too is why we are given revelation. It is interesting to notice that one of the reasons St. Thomas gives for the possibility that God did in fact reveal things to us is precisely that we might know this highest object in a way much more detailed than we might otherwise know it, though we can know of it in some sense from reason (I-II, 91, 4).

III.

"During this interview at Ashbourne, (September 23, 1777)," Boswell wrote, "Johnson and I frequently talked with wonderful pleasure of mere trifles which had occurred in our tour to the Hebrides; for it had left a most agreeable and lasting impression upon his mind."[6] Everything *that is*, that exists, I think, is designed ultimately to leave "a most agreeable and lasting impression" on our minds. Some of the greatest pleasures in things consist in remembering them, almost as if all things have second existences, first what they are, then our recollections of them. Moreover, the limitation of our lives, their time spans of seventy years and "eighty if we are strong," as the Psalm

6 Boswell, ibid., II, 150.

puts it, makes us realize that talking of the "wonderful pleasure of mere trifles" is limited ultimately not by the trifles or by the wonder but because of our own time span, almost as if to say that there is something lacking in our very memories, or perhaps in the expanse of our time, that requires fulfillment.

Those who are familiar with C. S. Lewis's space trilogy are aware, of course, that these novels were not really space fiction but theological considerations on the nature of man in the universe. Several people from Lord Acton to Douglas MacArthur and Henry Cardinal Manning are said to have remarked that, "at bottom, all political problems are theological." I suspect that this aphorism is in some sense true also of not only space fiction but of space exploration itself. Stanley Jaki has summed up what has come to be known as the "anthropomorphic principle": "The physical universe is indeed so lucid in its consistent workings as to suggest that it was tailored from the very start in such a specific way as to call for the eventual rise of man."[7] The shocking thing about the universe is not its size or time but its particularity, its "intelligent design," as it is called. If this is true, reality is rather more "fictitious" than fiction itself. The human race's "purpose" was evidently there from the beginning, as *Genesis* itself suggests. For it intimates that far from being an "accident," man was indeed "intended" in the very structure of the cosmos. There was a reason for him to exist that not merely added something to the cosmos itself, but explained the universe to itself, as if it were not sufficient for God to have explained it to Himself.

And yet, neither the cosmos nor man was created simply "for itself," but that both might "return" to what brought them forth. When St. Thomas begins the *Prima*

7 Stanley L. Jaki, "The Intelligent Christian's Guide to Scientific Cosmology," *Catholic Essays* (Front Royal, Va.: Christendom Press, 1990), 164.

Secundae of his *Summa Theologiae*, he talks of how the things that originally proceed from God, of which he spoke in the *Prima Pars*, return to their origin. He distinguishes those brings that have intelligence and will from those which do not. Only these former can return to God in any proper sense, and hence all other things return through the rational creatures because these latter have the capacity to know being, to know *what is*. Human happiness, then, is no small thing if its very end is the vision of the divine essence and this as a gift. This highest end almost makes it seem superfluous to talk of anything but God. And yet, what we emphasize here are the "small things" – the "other things on the face of the earth," as St. Ignatius called them – in the light of what is indeed the completion of our happiness.

If we read St. Thomas carefully about just what it is that finally defines our happiness, we will be surprised to notice how he describes the human being who in fact can know "whether God exists," even though he may not be fully sure what God is. With the help of revelation, St. Thomas knows that our happiness consists in seeing God "face to face." Stated philosophically, it means that we seek the face of the first cause that explains finite things, including ourselves. Here is how St. Thomas puts it:

> *Intellectus humanus, cognoscens essentiam alicuius effectus creati, non cognoscat de Deo nisi an est; nondum perfectio eius attingit simpliciter ad causam primam, sed remanet ei adhuc naturale desiderium inquirendi causam. Unde nondum est perfecte beatus. Ad perfectam igitur beatitudinem requiritur quod intellectus pertingat ad ipsam essentiam primae causae. Et sic perfectionem suam habebit per unionem ad Deum sicut ad objectum, in quo solo beatitudo hominis consistet* (I-II, 3, 8).[8]

---

8 "The human intellect, knowing the essence of some created effect, does not know anything of God except whether He exists; not yet has His perfection attained simply to the first cause, but there remains to him still the natural desire of inquiring about the [first] cause.

The human mind, then, does not know God directly. Knowing that created things are limited and not caused by themselves, the human intellect can know "whether" God exists, that is, that created things cannot cause or explain themselves. Knowing this, however, is perplexing. It is a cause of added unsettlement or intense curiosity. What about the nature of this "first cause?" Once being aware that something is there, it is impossible to rest content simply by knowing that such a cause exists. Yet, how this "union with God" might be possible is not available to the unaided human reason. But nothing is created in vain so that we should expect or anticipate or at least recognized once it is given, a solution, even if it does not arise from our own powers.

"But God does not do things by halves. He wanted to provide his creation with an image of His infinity," Yves Simon has written.

> He wanted certain creatures at least, in very unequal degrees to be sure but always on an admirable scale, to be infinite in some way, as He is infinite in all ways. But since every creature as it emerges from nothingness is reduced to the measure of its nature, and essentially limited to it, what was left to do was to endow the universe with a certain superabundance that allows privileged creatures to overcome their natural limitations – and even approach a kind of relative infinity – by being able to become in a sense all things. It is this superabundance of creation that makes things spill over into, or, better, radiate ideas. The universe of nature so generously created is at the same time the universe of intentionality, and that is how we are able to know it, and in knowing it imitate the divine infinity.[9]

Hence he is not yet perfectly happy. For perfect happiness, then, it is required that the intellect attain to the very essence of the first cause. And thus he [man] will have his perfection through union to God as to an object, in which alone the happiness of man consists."

9   Yves Simon, *An Introduction to Metaphysics of Knowledge*, trans. by V. Kuic and R. J. Thompson (New York: Fordham University Press, 1990), 24–25.

This passage from Simon is remarkable. What I am interested in here is not so much that man's final end consists in the vision of God face to face, but what is implied by this vision. Some religions or philosophies literally even want to absorb all individual beings into the Godhead, as if there is, in the end, only God. At first sight, it might seem that the knowledge of God absorbs all other interests into itself so that nothing else is needed. And yes, nothing else is needed. *Solus Deus.* Nevertheless, there is something "superabundant" about everything in creation, as if it is made both to be and to be known.

Chesterton, I think, captures the essence of what is at issue here in his book on St. Thomas. The remarkable thing about Christian revelation, Chesterton intimates, is not so much that it is concerned with God, but that God is concerned with everything He creates and so ought we to be. This means that nothing is without interest both in itself and to us. Here is how Chesterton put it:

> He [St. Thomas] was not a person who wanted nothing; and he was a person who was enormously interested in everything. His answer is not so inevitable or simple as some may suppose. As compared with many other saints, and many other philosophers, he was avid in his acceptance of Things; in his hunger and thirst for Things. It was his special spiritual thesis that there really are Things, and not only the Thing; that the many existed as well as the One.[10]

There really are things, and not just "the Thing." It is utterly distorted to want "nothing." We should be "enormously interested in everything." We should hunger and thirst after things. The many things did exist. The sum total of human happiness is located in these principles, in the little things that are there to be known precisely by us.

In this context, let me recall a passage from one of his Sermons, Pope St. Leo the Great observed:

10 G. K. Chesterton, *Saint Thomas Aquinas: The Dumb Ox* (Garden City, N.Y.: Doubleday Image, [1933] 1954), 135–36.

> Dear friends, at every moment *the earth is full of the mercy of God*, and nature itself is a lesson for all the faithful in the worship of God. The heavens, the sea and all that is in them bear witness to the goodness and omnipotence of their Creator, and the marvelous beauty of the elements as they obey him demands from the intelligent creature a fitting expression of its gratitude.[11]

The intelligent creature is to give a "fitting expression of its gratitude." For what? For precisely the reality and the goodness of things according to their manner. The gratitude follows on knowing what they are, on the "naming" of things, as it were.

If we recollect the passage cited in the beginning from St. Thomas's *De Veritate*, we will recall that, in knowledge, the perfection of one thing can be included in the perfection of another without changing the thing known. It is this superabundance of being that almost seems to demand that *what is* be also known. It is even more wondrous. St Thomas describes what might be the highest perfection that a human mind by its own powers might reach. The whole universe in its intelligible order can come to reside in a single intellect. "The entire order and causes of the universe" are inscribed in one soul. But notice that St. Thomas adds a remark from revelation. He does not deny that this exalted end is what the philosophers propose. He does not deny its wonder. But he adds a comment of Gregory the Great. "What do they not see who see Him who sees all things?" The answer, of course, is nothing.

Nonetheless, since we do not yet see Him who sees all things, we still see. The sum total of human happiness includes the seeing and the doing of all things rooted in *what is* that are not God. I will conclude with two instances of what I mean, one from Peanuts and one from Samuel Johnson.

11 St. Leo the Great, "Sermo 6 de Quadragesima," 1-2, *Roman Breviary*,
   Second Reading, Thursday after Ash Wednesday.

We see Charlie Brown watching Linus near a tree, sitting on the ground, a rather confused look on his face. Linus is piling rocks. Charlie asks, "What are you doing, Linus?" Linus responds, "Nothing." In the second scene, Charlie has come over closer to Linus. Charlie continues, "Nothing? It looks like you're building a rock wall." Linus replies, "What I meant was nothing important." In the third scene, we see Linus lining up the rock wall, while Charlie inquires, "Do you mind if I watch?" Suddenly, in the final scene, we realize Lucy has been listening to this, to her, idiotic conversation all along. To perplexed and put-down Charlie and Linus, she pronounces her judgment on the scene: "Fascinating . . . somebody useless watching somebody doing something unimportant." The amusement here, of course, reminds us of the delight of unimportant and useless things, the many things that just exist, the many actions that include someone watching someone else building stone walls.

On Good Friday, 1775, Boswell records attending St. Clement's Church with Samuel Johnson. In fact, they went to services both in the morning and in the evening. The morning preacher did not choose "a text appropriate for the day," but the afternoon preacher chose the most fitting text, "It is finished." They then return to Johnson's home where they have tea with Mrs. Williams, after which Johnson chats with Boswell for some time. Boswell speaks of his precise attention to what Johnson says. "My wish to hear him was such," Boswell remarks, "that I constantly watched every dawning of communication from that great and illuminated mind." It is as if all things are interesting, all things deserve illumination of mind.

In confirmation of this wonder of paying attention to those little things that, when added together, constituted the sum total of human happiness, Boswell records the following remark of Samuel Johnson:

> All knowledge is of itself of some value. There is nothing so minute or inconsiderable, that I would not

rather know it than not. In the same manner, all power [capacity], of whatever sort, is of itself desirable. A man would not submit to learn to hem a ruffle, of his wife, or his wife's maid; but if a mere wish could attain it, he would rather wish to be able to hem a ruffle.[12]

Nothing is so minute or inconsiderable that we would not wish to know it. We should like to be able to do all things if we did not have to go out of our way to learn them. The great things and the small things.

How could we not see all things "in Him who sees all things"? "The ultimate perfection achievable by the soul, according to the philosophers, is to have inscribed in it the entire order and causes of the universe." "Fascinating . . . somebody useless watching somebody doing something unimportant." "Ours is but a small matter in the great deeds of this time." It was St. Thomas's "special spiritual thesis that there really are Things, and not only the Thing, that the many existed as well as the One." "Sir, there is nothing too little for so little a creature as man." "A thing which is *not* God cannot be *except at the cost of not being what it is not*." The superabundance of all things enables us both to be ourselves but also to know what we are not. "The marvelous beauty of the elements as they obey Him demands from the intelligent creature a fitting expression of its gratitude."

---

12 *Boswell's Life of Johnson, ibid*, I, 590.

Chapter XIV

BELLOC'S SECOND WALK, A CENTURY LATER

"On the Character of Enduring Things"

"And on this account, Sussex, does a man love an old house, which was his father's, and on this account does a man come to love with all his heart, that part of earth which nourished his boyhood. For it does not change, or if it changes, it changes very little, and he finds in it the character of enduring things."

— Belloc, The Four Men, *Preface*[1]

The Path to Rome recounted the walk that Belloc took by himself from his old French army post in Toul to fulfill his vow to reach High Mass at St. Peter's in Rome on the Feast of Sts. Peter and Paul, the twenty-ninth of June. This walk, as we saw in the beginning, took place in 1901. The following year, 1902, Belloc records a second equally "wonder-full" walk that he took in his home county of Sussex in England. The termination of both these walks,

---

1 Hilaire Belloc, *The Four Men: A Farrago* (Oxford: Oxford University Press, 1984), xix.

one suspects, was the same, albeit one ending at St. Peter's, the other at his own home. On second thought the first walk did not exactly finish with Mass at St. Peter's. As he tells us, Belloc arrived when Mass was just ending. A priest told him in Latin that the next one would begin in twenty minutes. So he added twenty minutes to his pilgrimage and thus delightfully to his book.

During this extra time, Belloc, crossing St. Peter's Square, with no little amused irony, passed by an "Egyptian obelisk which the great Augustus had nobly dedicated to the Sun." "The Reader" then wanted to know, after all this wandering about Europe, whether he planned to say anything of Rome itself? "Nothing, dear Lector," Belloc retorted. Instead, while waiting, he went into a café down a long narrow street, where he "called for bread, coffee, and brandy." In the remaining few moments, he wrote doggerel verses summing up his now completed "Path" to Rome – "Drinking when I had a mind to, / Singing when I felt inclined to; / Nor ever turned my face to home / Till I had slaked my heart at Rome."

The Four Men also ends with verse: "When friend and fire and home are lost / And even children drawn away – / The passer-by shall hear me still, / A boy that sings on Duncton Hill." Belloc concludes the second walk simply, "full of these thoughts and greatly relieved by their metrical expression, I went, through the gathering darkness, southward across the Downs to my home." For Belloc, the kinship between home and Rome was not accidental.

The second walk lasts from the twenty-ninth of October to the second day of November, 1902. Included, in other words, with all their symbolisms, are All Hallows' Eve, All Hallows' Day, and All Souls' Day – the "Day of the Dead," as Belloc named it. These solemn days recall the human condition – we live, we sin, we repent, or perhaps we don't. From the beginning, what we are destined for, even if we do not reach it, is glory. But, as Belloc is aware, some there are, Pelagians all, who claim that they need no grace to attain such glory and are proudly confident that they can save themselves.

Later, outside the Crabtree Inn on the 31st of October, the four men, whom we shall soon meet, stop for beer and cheese. The Sailor decides to sing "in a very full and decisive manner" (48). The song that he chooses is marvelously entitled, "Song of the Pelagian Heresy for the Strengthening of Men's Backs and the very Robust Outthrusting of Doubtful Doctrine and the Uncertain Intellectual." No song-title is better suited to our time of doubtful doctrines and uncertain intellectuals who seek to accomplish everything, even their own salvation, for and by themselves.

Belloc gives the notes and the words of this little Pelagian tune. The words are remarkable: "Pelagius lived in Kardanoel, / And taught a doctrine there, / How whether you went to Heaven or Hell, / It was your own affair. / How, whether you found eternal joy / Or sank forever to burn, / It had nothing to do with the Church, my boy, / But was your own concern." One of the fellow walkers called this doctrine "blasphemous," but the Sailor maintained it was "orthodox," which it wasn't. He proceeded to sing the final "semi-chorus," as it is called: "Oh, he didn't believe / In Adam and Eve, / He put no faith therein! / His doubts began / With the fall of man, / And he laughed at original sin." The verses go on to recount the whole history of such heresy in song – no doubt the only way it should be studied. All utopias begin, I suspect, by this "laughing at original sin." They all end as a result by making things worse by "having nothing to do with the Church."

Belloc likewise records the tradition, not to be found specifically in *Genesis*, to be sure, that the Garden of Eden was originally found in his home county. On finishing this book, we can well believe it. He gives the following account of this local lore:

> When Adam was out (with the help of Eve) to name all
> the places of the earth (and that is why he had to live
> so long), he desired to distinguish Sussex, late his
> happy seat, by some special mark which would pick it
> out from all the other places of the earth, its inferiors
> and vassals. So that when Paradise might be regained
> and the hopeless generation of men permitted to pass
> the Flaming Sword at Shiremark Mill, and to see once
> more the four rivers, Arun and Adur, and Cuckmere
> and Ouse, they might know their native place again
> and mark it for Paradise (43).

The method Adam used to accomplish this special marking
of Paradise that is Sussex was that, in this county alone,
everything would be called by its opposite geographical
name. Down would be called Up, and North would be
called South. Moreover, "no one in the County should pro-
nounce 'th,' 'ph,' or 'sh,' but always 'h' separately, under
pain of damnation." For Belloc not only were Rome and
home identified, but both commenced in that Paradise
originally located in the county of Sussex, Belloc's own
county.

As I try to read T. S. Eliot's poem "Ash Wednesday"
every Ash Wednesday, so I endeavor to reread every year
Belloc's *Four Men* during these five "All Hallows'" days.
Belloc is right; enduring things are found here in this book,
including a certain sadness that always seems to be about
Belloc, in spite of his amazing jollity. Belloc, almost as
much as Plato, is poignantly aware of the passingness of
life and the need to attach what happens in time to more
eternal things. The Preface of *The Four Men* begins, "My
county, it has been proved in the life of every man that
though his loves are human, and therefore changeable, yet
in proportion as he attaches them to things unchangeable,
so they mature and broaden. On this account, Dear Sussex,
are those women chiefly dear to men who, as the seasons
pass, do but continue to be more and more themselves,
attain balance, and abandon or forget vicissitude." Belloc's

enduring things include the things he knew, the ones he loved, particularly the women.

The Four Men describes a walk through Sussex. The book includes maps, songs, sketches, and drawings. It is a perfect multi-media book and would make a wonderful film but only by a director wise enough not to change a word of the text. The sketches of the bridges, the stone buildings, the valleys are especially fine. The "four" men are each Belloc himself. They are called respectively, "Himself," "Grizzelbeard," "the Poet," and "the Sailor." In his complete life, Belloc of course was each of these men. He himself had sailed the seas, we remember the cruise of the Nona, written verses, and would grow old. He was a man who did not forget what he saw or knew. He loved companionship, but he also realized that it did not remain, however important it was while it lasted. "Himself" remarks to Grizzelbeard, after they agree to walk together, "for all companionship is good, but chance companionship is best of all . . ." (5). We shall return to the end of companionship when the four cease to walk together.

The walk began on October 29th, 1902, at an Inn, called the "George," at Robertsbridge. Alone, "Himself" sat drinking a glass of port. A "multitude of thoughts" came into his head but most importantly "the vision of the woods of home and of another place – the place where the [river] Arun rises." He talks to himself. He mocks himself that the purpose of his business far away seems to be only "to make money," the result of which he will return to spend more than he earns. What about ultimate things? He chides himself, "all the while your life runs past you like a river, and the things that are of moment to men you do not heed at all." The things that "are of moment to men" are indeed usually ignored until Belloc decides to walk in Sussex.

This is what *The Four Men* is about, the things that we should heed lest they run past us like a river. Or as he says to himself, "what you are doing is not worth while, and nothing is worth while on this unhappy earth except the

fulfillment of a man's desire." It is at this point in his soli-
tary broodings that "Himself" first meets Grizzelbeard, a
man "full of travel and of sadness." They also meet the
Sailor. They agree to walk together to the end of Sussex.
"This older man and I have inclined ourselves to walk
westward with no plan, until we come to the better parts of
the county, that is, to Arun and to the land I know,"
Himself explains to the Sailor.

As the walk begins, the three finally run into the fourth
companion, a youthful Poet. "His eyes were arched and
large as though in a perpetual surprise, and they were of a
warm grey colour. They did not seem to see the things
before them, but other things beyond; and while the rest of
his expression changed a little to greet us, his eyes did not
change. Moreover, they seemed continually sad."
Grizzelbeard, "as though he was his father," tells the Poet
that these three are good men. He will enjoy the walk.
"Only come westward with us and be our companion until
we go to the place where the sun goes down, and discover
what makes it so glorious" (16). Who could resist such a
destination, where the sun goes down, to discover "what
makes it so glorious?"

As they continue their walk through Sussex, each
recounts things he knew of the area. They know the geog-
raphy and lore of the place. The first story has to do with
St. Dunston. This is a wild narrative of how St. Dunston
tricked the Devil and thus caused a great moat to be built
in the land. Belloc includes some wise demonology, remi-
niscent of the lies that this same tainted gentleman told
our mother Eve in the Sussex Paradise: "And indeed this is
the Devil's way, always to pretend that he is the master,
though he very well knows in his black heart that he is
nothing of the kind" (19).

One of the remarkable things about Belloc is the place
that food plays in his life, vivid and concrete reminders of
our incarnational existence. He would certainly have dis-
dained and mocked modern dietary admonitions about cho-

lesterol and calories. My favorite Belloc meal is the following. The last light of the day had disappeared. "The air was pure and cold, as befitted All-Hallows." (146) The four men reached the edge of the Downs headed for the Hampshire border. Mist was on the Rother. They came to an old inn.

Sounds of singing from inside the inn greeted them. The men singing seemed to be farmers on a sales day. The bar of the inn was elegant. Some fifteen men were inside harmonizing and drinking. The four men were tired, and the other party would last long. The four were thus served at another table. What did they eat after their long day's march? The meal consisted

> of such excellence in the way of eggs and bacon, as we had none of us until that moment thought possible upon this side of the grave. The cheese also . . . was put before us, and the new cottage loaves, so that this feast, unlike any other feast that yet was since the beginning of the world, exactly answered all that the heart had expected of it, and we were contented and were filled (147).

I would hesitate to count the caloric intake here, but such a feast, "this side of the grave," in its description surely fulfills what Leon Kass, in his great book called, *Eating and the Perfecting of Our Nature.*[2]

After this feast, it was time for a pipe. Each called for his own drink. "Himself" had "black currant port." Grizzelbeard chose brandy. The Sailor bought the Poet beer, while the Sailor sipped claret. They then join the group of farmers. They sing together the rousing "Golier."

This scene recalls that wonderful institution, the inn. The Sailor, who has seen the world, remarks, "there is not upon this earth so good a thing as an inn; but even among good things there must be hierarchy" (62). The best inn in the world, we are told, was the Inn at Bramber; now for-

---

2 Leon Kass, *The Hungry Soul: Eating and the Perfecting of Our Nature* (New York: The Free Press, 1994).

gotten, it will not return. The great inns are listed. Their very names charm us and take us out of ourselves: the Star of Yarmouth, the Dolphin at Southhampton, the Bridge Inn of Amberley, the White Hart of Storrington, the Spread Eagle of Midhurst, "that oldest and most revered of all the prime inns of this world," the White Hart of Steyning, the White Horse of Storrington, and the Swan of Pentworth. Our business sees that these "were only mortal inns, human inns, full of a common and reasonable good; but round the Inn at Bramber, my companions, there hangs a very different air" (63). This is the inn of memory, so perfect that it cannot be visited again. "And what purpose would it serve to shock once more that craving of the soul for certitude and for repose?" Indeed, what purpose would it serve?

The conversation along the paths of Sussex is of battles and loves, of earthy things like fires and breakfast and ale. The best of ales is named in the Sailor's famous All Hallows' Day song: "May all good fellows that here agree / Drink Audit Ale in heaven with me, / And may all my enemies go to hell! / Noël! Noël! Noël! Noël!" (126). But amid this levity, we find an amazing profundity to their conversation.

> The mystery of how we stand to one another in the highest things comes back again and again. "Everything else that there is in the action of the mind save loving," Grizzelbeard points out, is of its nature a growth: it goes through its phases of seed, of miraculous sprouting, of maturity, of somnolescence, and of decline. But with loving it is not so; for the comprehension by one soul of another is something borrowed from whatever lies outside time: it is not under the confines of time. Then it passes, it is past – it never grows again: and we lose it as men lose a diamond, or as men lose their honour (27).

Himself objects that loss of honor is worse than loss of friends' love. Grizzelbeard did not think so. Honor is outside of us. We do not give it to ourselves. "Not so men who lose the affection of a creature's eyes. Therein for them, I mean in death, is no solution." What concerns Grizzelbeard is the mystery of the "passing of affection." Love is not under the confines of time, neither in its coming or in its going.

Belloc is never too far from warning us of the machinations of the academic and intellectual mind. "Himself" at one point remarks that "the Poet was now thoroughly annoyed, not being so companionable a man (by reason of his trade) as he might be. For men become companionable by working with their bodies and not with their weary noddles, and the spinning out of stuff from oneself is an inhuman thing" (123). We only know ourselves when we first know what is not ourselves.

On the final day, the four men arise early to end their chance companionship. They know they will never meet again. Grizzelbeard touchingly sums up their experience:

> There is nothing at all that remains: nor any house, nor any castle, however strong, nor any love, however tender and sound, nor any comradeship among men however hardy. Nothing remains but the things of which I will not speak, because we have spoken enough of them already during these four days. But I who am old will give you advice, which is this – to consider chiefly from now onward those permanent things which are, as it were, the shores of this age and the harbours of our glittering and pleasant but dangerous and wholly changeful sea (157–58).

Grizzelbeard speaks here of death. The four then pause "for about the time which a man can say good-bye with reverence." They go their own ways. Himself watches them depart "straining my sad eyes." He then returns to the Downs and his home.

CONCLUSION
ON ACKNOWLEDGING THE WONDER
OF *WHAT IS*

In Sussex, Belloc recalled, was found an old tradition that the Garden of Eden was once located there. But in Sussex also, Belloc finally returns home. He sees from a distance the smoke arising from the chimney of his home, just as Homer once recalled a similar scene. The "sum total of human happiness," I suspect, includes both home and the Garden. It was in the Garden, after all, that the Fall took place. That is, it happened in circumstances in which all was provided, as if to say that our main problem does not have to do with sufficiency of goods or shelter. The location of what is wrong with the world is not, ultimately, located outside of ourselves, though perhaps the solution for it. And this latter is what Incarnation, Salvation, Redemption are all about. They too are about gifts we must choose to receive.

Aquinas, in Chesterton's view, was a defender of the particularity of particular things. The world was created not only so that we could praise God but also that all that is good would receive its due. The fact that something stands outside of nothing is the ultimate fascination. But it is also the ultimate challenge. It is a matter of pride, the root of sin, that we refuse to praise anyone or anything but ourselves. But why does that which is not ourselves need praise? Things exist whether we praise them or not. Yet, there is an incompleteness in things when they are not acknowledged as good by whatever can recognize them as good. If we seek to be loved and affirmed, it is not a fault; it is merely an affirmation of what we are.

That everything *that is* should receive its proper acknowledgment is the thesis of this book. But only that can praise a thing, can stand in awe of a thing, which can also reject it. The drama of our existence is not merely that we are, but that we can respond to *what is* as if it might not be. I remain fascinated by the diversity of things, especially human things. I return to Socrates with his "longer road." We do seek the most important things. Yet, on the way we encounter everything else. *Solus Deus* is one very noble school of theology. *Omne quod est, est bonum* is another. If we rejoice in God because *He is*, we can likewise rejoice in everything else for the same reason, both that He is and that *what is, is*.

Josef Ratzinger was right to remind us that "love means being dependent on something that perhaps can be taken away from me." Chesterton was completely right in saying that love means our freely desiring to bind ourselves to what we love. This possibility of binding constitutes the main happiness of our lot in this world. God Himself is presented to us as "faithful." We can, indeed, as Augustine taught us, fall into error. We learn this by ourselves soon enough, to be sure. But it is not necessary that we remain there, in the error, unless we choose to do so.

But if we seek to escape from it, as we oftentimes do, we can only do so via the truth. The truth is what makes us free. We are not free just to be free. We are free to commit ourselves, to acknowledge the wonder of *what is*, of what is not ourselves. Chesterton again said that we want a world in which there is room both for gratitude and for wonder – gratitude because we know we did not make the world or ourselves, wonder because we are enchanted with the *what is* that is not ourselves or under our control.

Underneath the drama of the world lies, ultimately, not darkness but joy. It can be rejected, but it is there, even when rejected. The "haloes in Hell" attest to the fact that existence is, as such, a good thing. We can abuse what we are. We cannot doubt that what we are stands outside of nothingness. We know what it means to be here, in this passing world. The divine wisdom is, indeed, the cause of the "distinction in things." The universe would not be complete without its real variety. And it is this variety that is worth praising. To those who love God, all things work unto the good, as St. Paul told the Romans. It works to the good even of those who do not love God.

The sum total of human happiness – this is a reminder that we want more than ourselves to be happy, to achieve what it is to be a human being in this world, to be a human being designed in wonder, in mirth, in joy. The joy would not be worth having if we did not choose it.[1] Indeed, with Plato, it is difficult to see how the world could have been at all without those finite beings within it to praise it, praise it because *it is*, because they are, because they know that, ultimately, they are receivers of *what is*.

---

1 Peter Kreeft made the same point in another way: "But no one can make another person good by controlling their will, not even God." *The Philosophy of Tolkien* (San Francisco: Ignatius Press, 2004), 200.

BIBLIOGRAPHY

Arendt, Hannah, *The Human Condition*. New York: Doubleday Anchor, 1959.

Belloc, Hilaire, *The Four Men: A Farrago*. Oxford: Oxford University Press, 1984.

_____, *The Path to Rome*. Garden City, N.Y.: Doubleday Image, [1902] 1956.

Bloom, Allan, with Harry Jaffa, *Shakespeare's Politics*. Chicago: University of Chicago Press, 1964.

Boswell's Life of Johnson. London: Oxford, 1931. 2 vols.

Chesterton, G. K., *Collected Works*. San Francisco: Ignatius Press, 1986 to Present.

_____, *The Common Man*. New York: Sheed & Ward, 1950.

_____, *The Defendant*. London: Dent, [1901] 1914.

_____, *Heretics*. New York: John Lane, [1905] 1914.

_____, *Orthodoxy*. Garden City, N.Y.: Doubleday Image [1908] 1959.

_____, *Saint Thomas Aquinas The Dumb Ox*. Garden City, N.Y.: Doubleday Image, [1933] 1954.

Deane, Herbert, *Political and Social Ideas of St. Augustine*. New York: Columbia University Press, 1956.

George, Francis Cardinal, "One Lord and One Church for One World: The 10th Anniversary of *Redemptoris Missio. L'Osservatore Romano*. English, January, 2001.

Huizinga, Johan, *Homo Ludens: A Study of the Play-Element in Culture*. Boston: Beacon Press [1930] 1955.

Jaki, Stanley L., *Catholic Essays*. Front Royal, Va.: Christendom Press, 1990.

Kass, Leon, *The Hungry Soul: Eating and the Perfection of Our Nature*. Chicago: University of Chicago Press, 1994.

Kraynak, Robert P., *Christian Faith and Modern Democracy: God and Politics in the Fallen World*. Notre Dame, Ind.: University of Notre Dame Press, 2001.

Kreeft, Peter, *The Philosophy of Tolkien*. San Francisco: Ignatius Press, 2004.

Langan, Thomas, *The Catholic Tradition*. Columbia: University of Missouri Press, 1998.

Lewis, C. S., *The Problem of Pain*. New York: Macmillan, 1962.

_____, *The Weight of Glory and Other Addresses*. New York: Macmillan, 1980.

Mahoney, Daniel, *Solzhenitsyn: The Ascent from Ideology*. Lanham, Md.: Rowman & Littlefield, 2001.

Maritain, Jacques, *Approches sans entraves*, in *Oeuvres Complètes Maritain*. Paris: Editions St. Paul, 1991.

McInerny, Ralph, *The Very Rich Hours of Jacques Maritain: A Spiritual Life*. Notre Dame, Ind.: University of Notre Dame Press, 2003.

New Yorker Cartoon Album: 1975–1985. New York: Viking,

1985.

Newman, John Henry, *The Idea of a University*. Garden City, N.Y.: Doubleday Image, 1959.

Nietzsche, Friedrich, *Beyond Good and Evil*. Translated by R. J. Hollingsdale. Harmondsworth, England: Penguin, 1972.

Pascal, Blaise, *Pensées*. New York: Modern Library, 1941.

Pernoud, Régine, *Those Terrible Middle Ages*. San Francisco: Ignatius Press, 2000.

Pieper, Josef, *The Concept of Sin*. South Bend, Ind.: St. Augustine's Press, 2001.

————, *Happiness and Contemplation*. Translated by Richard and Clara Winston. New York: Pantheon, 1958; South Bend, Ind.: St. Augustine's Press, 1998.

————, *Josef Pieper – an Anthology*. San Francisco: Ignatius Press, 1989.

————, *Leisure: The Basis of Culture*. Translated by G. Malsbary. South Bend, Ind.: St. Augustine's Press, 1998.

————, *Living the Truth (The Truth of All Things* and *The Right and the Good)*. San Francisco: Ignatius Press, 1989.

Poor H. Allen Smith's Almanac: A Comic Compendium Loaded with Wisdom & Laughter, together with a Generous Lagniappe of Questionable Natural History, All Done Up in Style. Greenwich, Conn.: Fawcett, 1965.

Ratzinger, Josef Cardinal, *Dominus Jesus. L'Osservatore Romano*, English, September 6, 2000.

————, *Salt of the Earth: The Church at the End of the Millennium*. An Interview with Peter Seewald. San Francisco: Ignatius Press, 1997.

Royal, Robert, *Catholic Martyrs of the Twentieth Century*. New York: Crossroads, 2000.

Schall, James V., *Far Too Easily Pleased: A Theology of Play, Contemplation, and Festivity*. Los Angeles:

Benziger/Macmillan, 1976.

_____, *On the Unseriousness of Human Affairs: Teaching, Writing, Playing, Believing, Lecturing, Philosophizing, Singing, Dancing.* Wilmington, Del.: ISI Books, 2001.

Schulz, Charles, *Don't Be Sad, Flying Ace.* New York: Topper, 1990.

_____, *Let's Face It, Charlie Brown.* New York: Fawcett, 1959.

Schumacher, E. F., *A Guide for the Perplexed.* New York: Harper Colophon, 1977.

Simon, Yves, *A General Theory of Authority.* Notre Dame, Ind.: University of Notre Dame Press, 1980.

_____, *An Introduction to the Metaphysics of Knowledge.* Translated by V. Kuic and R. J. Thompson. New York: Fordham University Press, 1990.

Sokolowski, Robert, "The Method of Philosophy: Making Distinctions," *The Review of Metaphysics*, LI (March, 1998), 515–32.

Strauss, Leo, *Thoughts on Machiavelli.* Glencoe, Ill.: The Free Press, 1958.

Tolkien, J. R. R., *The Return of the King.* New York: Ace, n. d.

_____, *The Two Towers.* New York: Act, 1965.

Voegelin, Eric, *Science, Politics, and Gnosticism.* Chicago: Regnery.1968.

Waugh, Evelyn, *A Little Learning: An Autobiography.* Boston: Little, Brown, 1964.

Wojtyla, Karol (Pope John Paul II), *Crossing the Threshold of Hope.* New York: Knopf, 1994.

INDEX